The facts....................ports
in the pub..................
are taken fro................ords where
available, rec..............ents from those
involved, local n........per and media reports,
the internet and other reference works and
biographies. Over time some of the occurrences
may have been exaggerated or embellished.
Any parts of the book not verified by being in
the public record must be treated as allegations.

Published by BSA Publishing 2023 who
assert the right that no part of this may be
stored in a retrieval system, reproduced or
transmitted without the prior permission of
the publisher.
Copyright @ B.L.Faulkner 2023 who
asserts the moral right to be identified as
the author of this work
Cover Peter Swain at Orphan Printers

ISBN 9781739565732

# AMERICAN KILLERS

## Volume 1. ALABAMA

**A majority of American states have the death penalty, but far fewer use it regularly.** As of the date of publishing this book, the death penalty is authorized by 27 states and the federal government – including the U.S. Department of Justice and the U.S. military – and prohibited in 23 states and the District of Columbia. But even in many of the jurisdictions that authorize the death penalty, executions are rare: 13 of these states, along with the U.S. military, haven't carried out an execution in over ten years, this includes three states – California, Oregon and Pennsylvania – where governors have imposed formal moratoriums on executions.

Authors note. Being an English author of true crime and crime fiction please note that the spelling of certain words is different in the UK from the USA. For instance, defense/defence, check/cheque etc. and make allowances for this. Not every killer in the State is included as some murders are pretty basic accidents or arguments that got out of control. I have tried to keep to those with unusual or interesting back grounds that led to the crime so not every convicted killer will be in the book. I am always pleased to hear from readers on my Facebook page. I don't have a website, it is too time consuming.

# JOSEPH DEWEY AKIN

Born 1956 – March 1998 pleaded guilty to manslaughter and sentenced to 15 years.

Akin worked as a nurse at Cooper Green Hospital in Birmingham, Alabama and was first tried in September 1992 for the murder of Robert Price, a quadriplegic, but injecting him with a lethal amount of lidocaine. Akin was suspected of foul play in nearly a hundred other deaths over the previous decade in the various hospitals where he had worked. When the management of these hospitals attention had later been drawn to the fact that Akin was always present at these deaths they had refused to investigate for fear of litigation.

In the Robert Price case the amount of lidocaine found in Price's body was twice a lethal dose and four times more than would usually be prescribed as a medical dose. Atkin's defence lawyer at his trial in 1992 pointed out that the initial cardiac arrest was caused by a blocked ventilation tube with no evidence Akin had tampered with that tube. He also pointed out that the lidocaine was administered by the Code Blue emergency team as they tried to save Price's life. The drug had originally been invoiced to Price's family which meant it had been ordered by the hospital for his treatment and not brought in by Akin.

Akin was found guilty of murder but this conviction was overturned and a retrial ordered which failed to reach a verdict. A third trial was due in March 1998 but Akin changed his plea to guilty of manslaughter before it began and was found guilty on that charge and sentenced to 15 years.

The suspicious deaths at other hospitals where Akin worked lay open on the police files and several payouts have been made in the civil court by Akin's insurance company and by some of those hospitals to relatives of his suspected victims under threat of court proceedings.

# TOMMY ARTHUR

Born 1942- sentenced to death December 5$^{th}$ 1991. Executed May 26$^{th}$ 2017.

This is a strange case. On February 1$^{st}$ 1982 Arthur was found guilty of killing Troy Wicker who he shot through the right eye. At the time Arthur was having an affair with Judy Wicker, the victim's wife, who had colluded with other relatives to hire Arthur for $10,000 to kill Troy. After the killings Judy told the police that her husband had been killed by an Afro-American burglar who had beaten and raped her. This was Arthur who had blacked his face and wore a wig in collusion with Judy to confuse any witnesses. Both he and Judy were seen together after the murder as he made his getaway. Arthur was arrested and charged with murder and found guilty. The conviction was overturned on appeal in 1983.

Arthur had a previous conviction from 1977 for killing his sister-in-law, again by shooting her through the eye. His conviction was postponed for many years after his lawyers filed motions that the Alabama method of execution by lethal injection was cruel as it would cause Arthur severe pain due to his heart condition. You couldn't make it up could you? The court had no alternative but to postpone Arthur's execution as his lawyers posted appeal after appeal and each wound its slow way through the various courts. It was only after the Supreme Court lifted the stay of execution in 2017, after the state governor had ordered a new drug that was designed to render the inmate unconscious before the lethal dose was administered, that Arthur was given the lethal execution drugs and was pronounced dead at 12.15am on May 26$^{th}$ 2017.

# BRIAN K BALDWIN

Born June 16$^{th}$ 1958 – executed in Alabama June 18$^{th}$ 1999.

Baldwin is typical of the cases involving racial prejudice and injustice that occurred in Alabama in the late 1900's. He was accused aged 18, together with accomplice Edward Horsley, of the murder of 16 year old Naomi Rolon after they fled a North Carolina prison camp in March 1977, stole a car and abducted Naomi who was on her way to pay a hospital visit to her father. She was choked, stabbed and sexually assaulted as they drove to Alabama before killing her with an axe.

Several inconstancies in the prosecution's actions and statements were placed before the Alabama Governor Don Seigleman who said he was deeply troubled by them but refused to give clemency on the execution day. The defence lawyers claimed Baldwin was beaten into confessing in a state dominated by white lawmen and officers. Baldwin was refused his right to a fair and impartial trial, his right to be free from torture and his right to be free from racial discrimination. The defence noted the following issues;

*After his arrest Baldwin's parents were not informed of his whereabouts until after he had been convicted of capital murder.*

*Baldwin was repeatedly beaten and prodded by an electric 'cattle-prodder' until he signed a confession.*

*This confession did not originally provide an accurate description of the murder or of the weapon used. This confession was later altered to fit.*

*The trial lasted just one and a half days including jury selection where all coloured potential jurors were rejected by the prosecution, jury deliberation and sentencing.*

*Baldwin's attorney failed to conduct a pre-trial investigation, failed to prepare Baldwin to testify, failed to call any defence witnesses, failed to produce any exculpatory forensic evidence and failed to raise objections to the prosecution's improper actions and allegations.*

*Forensic evidence that pointed towards Baldwin being innocent was not introduced at the trial.*

*Baldwin was in the courtroom in handcuffs during jury selection.*

*The prosecution mentioned sexual assault by Baldwin on many occasions although it was not on the charge sheet.*

*After the trial the state withheld the record of the trial and claimed to have lost key evidence from Baldwin's defence which hindered the setting up of an appeal.*

*Baldwin's co-defendant confessed to the crime and exonerated Baldwin.*

In a county where 46% of the population were African-Americans it was an all white jury that convicted Baldwin.

An Alabama court later examined the trial and concluded that the prosecutor and judge had shown 'deliberate racial bias and discrimination'.

Co-defendant Edward Horsley, a white man, was not convicted although forensic evidence showed none of Rolon's blood on Baldwin's clothes but much of it on

Horsley's. The axe used in the killing was struck from the left, Horsley was left handed, Baldwin was right handed. Horsley had driven off with Rolon leaving Baldwin alone. Eleven years after Baldwin had been executed Horsley confessed to killing Naomi Rolon alone and stated that Baldwin knew nothing about the murder until Rolon's body had been found.

It beggars belief that the initial appeal alleging improper court procedure and racism was heard by the same judge that had convicted Baldwin and against whom some of those allegations were being made! He, not surprisingly, refused the appeal.

Brian Baldwin was sat, strapped in the electric chair for one hour whilst his lawyers made unsuccessful last ditch appeals for clemency and a retrial to the Alabama Governor who refused them. The switch was then thrown.

# THOMAS E BLANTON Jr

Born 1939 – sentenced to life in prison May 2$^{nd}$, 2001.

On the morning of September 15$^{th}$ 1963, a bomb exploded in the Sixteenth Street Baptist Church in Birmingham, Alabama killing four coloured girls who were changing into their choir robes in the basement and injuring twenty other people. The church was an important part of the local African-American community and a meeting place for civil rights activists both black and white. Martin Luther King Jr was just one of many leaders who had visited and spoken at the church meetings.

Bomb and fire threats had been made against the church in the past and precautions were always taken, but this time no threat had been received. The blast blew a hole in the east side of the church and brought down ceilings and walls. The four girl's bodies were found as the local community dug through the debris in the search for survivors.

The FBI led the investigation and in 1965 named Robert Chambliss, Bobby Cherry, Herman Cash and Thomas E Blanton Jr as the bombers, all were known members of the Ku Klus Klan. The Birmingham FBI wanted to prosecute but did not. Years later it was revealed in FBI papers that Edgar J Hoover had blocked the prosecutions and by 1968 no charges had been brought and the case was dropped and closed.

In 1971 public unease and continued agitation at the lack of action forced the Alabama Attorney General William Baxley to reopen the case. It plodded on slowly through the courts until on November 18th 1977 Robert Chambliss was convicted of murder and sentenced to life in prison. In 1988 evidence was sent to the FBI by way of an anonymous tip off that Herman Cash was one of the bombers but he died in 1994 before a case could be heard against him. On May 17th 2000 Thomas E. Blankton Jr and Bobby Cherry were charged with the murder of the four girls. Cherry's trial was postponed when the judge ruled that he was mentally incompetent to stand trial. Another judge challenged this and Cherry was found competent and on May 22nd 2002 he was found guilty of the murders and sentenced to life in prison.

Previously on May 17th 2000 Thomas E. Blanton Jr was charged with the murders and on May 1st the following year, 2001, he was convicted and sentenced to life in prison. This conviction rested mainly on secret FBI recordings of conversations between Blanton and his wife where he discussed being at a Klan meeting where the bombing was planned and the bomb made. In another he was recorded talking to a person who he was unaware was a FBI informant and admitting his part in the bombing. Those taped conversations were played to the jury in court and sealed his guilt. Finally justice had been served for the four girls.

# WILLIAM GLENN BOYD

Born January 6$^{th}$ 1966 – executed by lethal injection March 31$^{st}$ 2011

William Boyd together with his friend, Robert Milstead broke into the home of Fred Blackmon, 76, and his wife Evelyn, 41, on the afternoon of March 26$^{th}$ 1986 and tied them up before convincing them that they had kidnapped Evelyn's daughter and would kill her unless the Blackmon's paid a ransom.

Fred was accompanied to his bank at gunpoint and withdrew $5,000. Both he and his wife were then driven to some local woods on the pretext of the daughter being there and both were beaten and then shot dead. Boyd and Milstead left the scene only to return later to dispose of the bodies. A police search was made after the Blackmons were reported missing by relatives and both Boyd and Milstead were identified by witnesses and the bank staff as being with the Blackmons on the last day they were seen. Forensic evidence at the Blackmon's home was also linked to the pair who were arrested on suspicion of kidnap and murder.

Robert Milstead struck a plea deal in exchange for his testimony incriminating Boyd and led the police to the bodies. Fred's body was found inside the boot of his car which had been driven off the bank into the Coosa River. Evelyn's body was also recovered from the river inside a metal drum. Her body had been roughly dismembered by an axe to make it fit inside the drum.

Boyd was convicted of the murder and given the death sentence by the judge who overruled the jury's request for clemency and a life sentence. Milstead received a life sentence without parole as part of his plea deal which the judge could not overrule.

A last minute appeal for a retrial by Boyd's attorneys citing that the judge had no legal right to overrule the jury's request for leniency was denied and Boyd was 45 when he was given a lethal injection on March 31$^{st}$, 2011, twenty five years after the double murders. Death row moves very slowly as appeals up the chain of the court system in the USA overwhelmed it and it hardly moves at all.

# DANNY JOE BRADLEY

Born 7th September 1959 – executed February 12th 2009 by lethal injection.

On January 24th 1983, twelve year old Rhonda Hardin and her younger brother Gary were at their home being looked after by their step father Danny Bradley as their mother Judy Bradley was in hospital. During the evening they were visited by three friends of the family, Jimmy Isaac, John Bishop and Dianne Mobley who left the home at about 8pm leaving the two children and Bradley watching television. Gary decided to go to bed and was told by Bradley not to wake Rhonda who had fallen asleep on the sofa.

Around midnight Bradley went to his father-in-law's house and told him Rhonda had disappeared and he was out looking for her. At approximately 1am Bradley called at his neighbour, Philip Manus's house and told him that he and Rhonda had argued over some medicine she was supposed to take after which he had fallen asleep in the living room and when he awoke Rhonda was nowhere to be found. Manus wanted to call the police but Bradley insisted they go to the hospital and tell Judy Bradley first. It took nearly 3 hours before they were able to see Judy Bradley who was under sedation and when they did she told them to call the police. This they finally did, reporting Rhonda missing and then they returned at approximately 7.30am to Manus's house. The police search discovered Rhonda's body in some woodland about half a mile from her home. She was dressed in a pair of maroon corduroy trousers, leg warmers, a red knitted jumper, a bra, a blue windbreaker and tennis shoes with the laces tied by a single knot. At the later trial Judy Bradley insisted that Rhonda always tied her shoes with a double knot.

Bradley was held for questioning although not having been arrested or charged. He maintained he had not left his home until he went to his father-in-law's house and then Philip Manus's house although an officer who had known him for twenty years had seen him in his car earlier near the woods at 9.30pm that evening.

Forensic searches matched fibres from Rhonda's clothing to those found in Bradley's car boot. Semen from Bradley's blood group was found in Rhonda's rectum, vagina and on her clothes and other material in her bedroom.

Bradley was charged with murder and explained that he had been out looking for a car to steal when seen earlier that night by the officer who recognised him. The evidence was conclusive as far as the jury were concerned and they found him guilty of first degree murder of Rhonda Hardin during the commission of rape and sodomy and recommended by twelve to zero that he be sentenced to death.

As usual with death row the appeals wound there way slowly through the courts until finally the U.S. Supreme Court denied any further stay of execution and opened the way for Bradley's execution which took place 26 years after the guilty verdict on February 12$^{th}$ 2009. He had two fried egg sandwiches as a last meal and had nothing to say to those attending.

# GARY LEON BROWN

Born July 14th 1958 – executed by lethal injection April 24th. 2003.

On May 26th, 1986, Gary Brown 18, Archie Bankhead 19, James Bynum 21, and Jimmy Davenport 19, went fishing near Locust Fork, Alabama, thirty miles from Birmingham. During the day they drank a lot of alcohol and continued drinking that evening at Chuck and Willies Lounge in Birmingham where they hatched a plan to rob a local gay man, Jack McGraw, at his trailer home in Pinson. All had recently received payments from McGraw for performing sexual acts with him. McGraw was thought to be wealthy with his money hidden somewhere in his trailer.

They drove to McGraw's and whilst Davenport stayed in the car the other three knocked at the trailer door and were let inside by McGraw who declined the offer to go drinking with them as he was on an early shift at his workplace the next morning. McGraw walked outside with them when they left and was grabbed in a headlock by Bankhead. Davenport later stated he saw Brown and Bynum hitting McGraw and Brown slashing at his neck with a knife. McGraw fell to the ground and the trio dragged him back inside the trailer. Afraid he would identify them to the police they decided to kill him and Brown stabbed him repeatedly 78 times with a penknife. McGraw's neck was slashed which resulted in his death by loss of blood from the carotid artery.

They then ransacked McGraw's home and put anything of value into the car and took it to Bankhead's house where they split it between them and shared the money in McGraw's wallet, just $67. They then changed their clothes burning their old ones which were covered in McGraw's blood in the backyard.

McGraw's body was found the next day by a young neighbour who noticed the trailer door swinging open. It did not take long for the Jefferson County Sheriffs to arrest the three killers who admitted the theft of McGraw's belongings but blamed each other for the murder. Forensic evidence of their burnt clothes in Bankhead's backyard and McGraw's property in their possession as well as Bankhead's wife testifying that she heard them discussing the killing was enough for murder charges to be brought against them. Davenport was also arrested and then released without charge when it became clear he was the driver and had no part in the murder.

The prosecution called for the death penalty for all three. Brown was given the death penalty but Bankhead and Bynum received life in prison sentences after Brown admitted to being the one who had the knife and stabbed McGraw. Bankhead's sentence remains in force, Bynum has been paroled in 1997.

Once again Brown's appeals slowly worked their way through the courts until 2002 when Brown was due to die in the electric chair but the Supreme Court stayed his execution at the last hour on the grounds put forward by human rights organisations that the electric chair was an inhuman and cruel punishment. On April 24$^{th}$ 2003, Gary Brown then age 44, was executed after the Governor Bob Riley, who had the sole right to grant clemency to death row prisoners in Alabama, denied it.

# RAYMOND EUGENE BROWN

Born 1946 – sentenced to three life terms in 1960 for a triple murder. Paroled in 1973. The parole revoked in 1980 after an assault. Paroled again 1986. Parole revoked 1987after committing another murder.

Raymond Brown was just 14 years old in October 1960 when he used a six-inch knife to murder his 83-year-old great-grandmother, his 63-year-old grand-mother and his 31-year-old great-aunt. He had entered their house to steal enough money to buy a new pair of trainers. He was barefoot and disturbed when his grand-mother awoke to find him in her room and called out to the others. The post-mortems found 123 stab wounds in the three victims and bloody footprints left by Brown as he fled the scene. Quickly arrested Brown maintained he could not remember anything about that night but confessed to the killings to avoid a death sentence and although just 14 years old he was tried and convicted as an adult and given life in prison. After just 12 years he was paroled in 1973 and using the skills learnt on a mechanic's course whilst in prison he was employed at a garage at Ashland, Alabama and rented a small apartment in Montgomery. In 1980 he attempted to rape the female manager of the apartment block and when she resisted he tried to strangle her but was unsuccessful and was arrested, his parole was revoked and he was returned to prison.

In 1986 he was once again paroled, he must have had a great lawyer to be able to convince the parole board he was a fit and proper person to be released back into the public domain again. But paroled he was. He worked as a vehicle mechanic in Phoenix City where he began dating divorcee Linda LeMonte, 32. He was a regular at her apartment and according to the neighbours was well liked by everyone including LeMonte's 10 year old daughter Sheila and 6 year old son Aaron. On the morning of August 10$^{th}$ 1987, LeMonte's boss phoned her mother Beverly Evans to say he was worried as Linda had not come to work and was not answering her phone. Evans checked the children's school who said that neither of them had come to school that day. Evans and her husband went to Linda LeMonte's house and when they got no answer at the door they walked around and knocked on the back windows. When they knocked on six year old Aaron's bedroom window he crawled out from hiding under his bed and opened the front door.

They found Linda LeMonte lying dead on the floor in the lounge and ten year old Sheila dead in her bedroom. The medical examiner's report later stated that a nine inch cut to her throat had killed Linda and Sheila had multiple stab wounds with the knife still embedded in her stomach. Both had been sexually assaulted with Linda having her breasts stabbed several times and a long cut from her throat to her vagina which was deep enough to expose her abdominal cavity and internal organs. The killer had taken a Polaroid photo of the body and left it on top of the television. Brown's fingerprint was found on this photo.

The search for Brown, now 41, began in earnest. He was not at his apartment although traces of Linda LeMonte's blood were found on clothes there. The public were warned that he was 'a psychopathic killer who killed for pleasure, very dangerous' and not to approach him

One piece of good luck was that Brown did not have a vehicle or he could have been anywhere in the USA. He had been involved in a traffic accident whilst drunk the day before the murders and his vehicle had been impounded.

Brown managed to evade capture for two days by living rough but was recognised by a gas station attendant in Wellsboro when he went in to buy food and drink and was arrested on the premises.

At the run up to his trial for the murder of Linda LeMonte and her daughter the Alabama Pardons and Parole Board took a lot of flack for releasing Brown on parole twice, once to kill again. The verdict was guilty and the sentence was death but the defence argued that the publicity about his previous murders would have made it impossible to have an unbiased jury to be selected for the trial. This observation led to a twelve year argument through the courts appeal system that went as far as the Supreme Court before the original verdict was upheld and Brown was executed in Alabama in 1988.

# JAMES HARVEY CALLAHAN

Born 1947 – executed by lethal injection January 15$^{th}$ 2009

On February 3$^{rd}$ 1982, Becky Howell, a 26 year old student at Jacksonville State University went to watch her fiancé, Murray Knight, and his band, play at a local club. During the set Howell went across the road to a launderette to do her laundry. She never returned to the club and after his band had finished playing Knight went across to the launderette searching for her. He found her books and laundry but no trace of Becky. Knight called the police.

It took two weeks until Becky was found dead in Tallasseehatchee Creek in Calhoun County, Alabama. She had been strangled, her hands were taped together, her belt on upside down and she was not wearing her pantyhose, shoes or socks. A vaginal swab found the presence of semen.

Police appeals and reconstructions brought forward a witness, Jimmy Dunagan, on the 20$^{th}$ February. Dunagan was parked along from the launderette on the night Becky disappeared and noticed a green Ford pick-up outside the launderette and had noted the driver watching a young lady in a phone box and pulling along next to her when she left the booth. The lady had run to her car and driven to the Jackson State University Campass followed by the green pick-up and Dunagan who had noted its number. The pick-up belonged to James Callahan a known criminal who was on probation at that time for Assault with Intent to Murder. The pick-up was found outside James

Callahan's father's residence on 21st February and identified by Dunagan as the one he had followed from the launderette on February 3rd. James Callahan was arrested and a pistol, a pillow and two pairs of jeans were found inside his pick-up. Callahan gave four conflicting statements concerning his movements on the night of the 3rd February with none able to be confirmed by a reliable witness.

Callahan admitted being an ex-boyfriend of Becky Howell and had seen her at the launderette that night. He said they had gone back to his trailer and had sex and then gone for a drive. When they were driving through the woods near Tallasseehatchee Creek Becky had jumped from the truck and run off in her bare feet.

Forensic evidence linked Callahan's fingerprints to the tape binding Becky's wrists and her hair strands were found in the truck plus fibres from carpet in Callahan's trailer were found on her clothes. The semen was found on a vaginal swab which matched his secretor group. The medical examiners also testified that Becky's feet and ankles were unscathed and had she run through the bracken and undergrowth barefoot at Tallasseehaychee Creek as Callahan stated they would have been scratched and cut.

On June 26th 1982 Callahan was convicted of intentionally murdering Rebecca Suzanne Howell during the course of a first degree kidnapping, a capital offence. The jury found him guilty by a 10 to 2 vote and he received the death sentence. The Alabama Supreme Court reversed the decision and a new trial was ordered which passed another guilty verdict. More appeals were lodged claiming misuse of police protocols when interviewing Callahan without legal representation and prosecution evidence used that should have been inadmissible at the trial.

These legal arguments dragged on until 2009 when his lawyers exhausted all the avenues of appeal and the U.S. Supreme Court upheld the death sentence. Callahan was executed by lethal injection in Alabama on January 15$^{th}$ 2009 after a last meal of two corn dogs, French fries and a Coke. He bequeathed $36.42 to his son plus two watches, a Walkman, a radio and some clothes.

# MARIO GIOVANNI CENTOBIE

Born January 26$^{th}$, 1966 – executed by lethal injection 28$^{th}$ April, 2005.

In 1995, for some inexplicable reason, Mario Centobie decided to kidnap his ex-wife and son. They were in a protection scheme because of his previous domestic violence towards them both and he had a ban in force on visiting or contacting them. They escaped from him and when he was arrested he claimed they had accompanied him voluntarily. The judge and jury took a different view and Centobie was sent down for 40 years.

In 1998 whilst being transferred between jails he and another convict named Jeremy Granberry, 19, managed to overpower their guards and escape in the car. The two guards were found the next day tied to the posts of an old tumble down barn.

Centobie and Granberry drove into Alabama where police Captain Cecil Lancaster noted the marked prison vehicle on Interstate 359 that had the rear bumper missing and pulled it over. Centobie shot Lancaster twice as the officer approached the car. One bullet was stopped by the buckle on his belt and the second one hit two of his ribs before exiting through his back. The pair drove on to Birmingham and two days later were pulled over in Moody by Officer Keith Turner on a routine traffic stop. Centobie shot Turner three times including a bullet in the head which killed him.

On July 5$^{th}$ 1998 Granberry and Centobie split up with Granberry being caught the next day whilst Centobie evaded capture for a week by carjacking a Moody man's car and forcing him to drive to

Mississippi. The man managed to escape at a rest area where Centobie hitched a lift with an unsuspecting tourist family in their mobile home. Alerted by the carjacked driver the police caught up with the vehicle two exits further down the interstate and Centobie was arrested without resisting although he still had the gun with him.

Three months later whilst being held on remand for murder at Etowah County Maximum Security Jail he escaped again! This time by convincing a female warder that he loved her and promising her marriage if she helped him escape, which she did. He was caught in Atlanta two weeks later after writing love letters to the female warder that he stupidly posted close to the trailer he was hiding in.

Centobie was sent to trial and convicted of the murder of Officer Keith Turner and sentenced to death on January 8$^{th}$ 1999. An appeal was dismissed and on his own orders to his defence lawyers they did not pursue further appeals to higher courts.

Centobie was executed by lethal injection in Holman prison Alabama at 6pm on 28$^{th}$ April, 2005 age 39. His last meal at 3 pm was barbecue chicken, egg noodles with butter, turnip greens, candid sweet potatoes and a strawberry soda. He had no final words for the witnesses to the execution.

## ROBERT EDWARD CHAMBLISS.

See Thomas E Blanton Jr.. Chambliss was convicted of murder along with Blanton and sentenced to several life in prisonment terms. He died in prison in 1985 still claiming his innocence.

## BOBBY FRANK CHERRY

See Thomas E Blanton Jr. Cherry was convicted of the Sixteenth Street Baptist Church Bombing that killed four young coloured girls. He boasted about 'lighting the fuse' to his wife who testified against him. He died of cancer in prison age 74 on November 18$^{th}$ 2004.

## WILLIE CLISBY Jr.

Born 1948 – executed by electrocution April 28$^{th}$ 1995.

This is another capital case that meandered through the various appeal courts until the final appeal was dismissed by the Supreme Court of Appeals and the original death sentence was finally carried out.

On November 5$^{th}$, 1979, Willie Clisby Jr., age 31, broke into the home of Fletcher Handley, a 58 year old handicapped man who he worked with at a local cemetery in Birmingham, Alabama, and killed him with an axe stealing just $80.

Clisby was tried, convicted of murder and sentenced to death in 1981. The defence then set in motion a series of appeals. They contested that Clisby was suffering from a mental disorder and had been denied the medical resources to prove his mental illness. That was contested by the prosecution medical team. The defence said that the prosecution medics were not experienced enough to rule in the case and their psychiatric evidence was faulty. These appeals took time and were all dismissed. The last one being that to electrocute Clisby would be inhuman, cruel and cause excess pain.

Clisby, then 47, was finally executed by electrocution in Alabama on April 28th, 1995.

# EARL LEWELLYN DAUGHTREY Jr.

Born 22$^{nd}$ December 1950 – died 27$^{th}$ June 2008 age 57. Never convicted but publicly declared a suspect in 3 murders that are still under investigation.

Daughtrey's violent streak surfaced when he was accused of trying to choke a female class mate at their high school in Berrien County. No charges were brought and he left school soon after to find work. Daughtrey married in 1971 and moved to Anniston, Alabama taking jobs in construction. Three months into this work Daughtrey was part of a construction team landscaping the home of Harvey and Betty Refroe in Lincoln when Betty was found dead on the kitchen floor. She was partially clothed and strangled by one of husband Harvey's shirts knotted around her neck.

Harvey Refroe was convicted of the murder mainly on the testimony of a local sheriff. That officer was later impeached and sacked for embezzlement, false witness and violence. Harvey's defence appealed and won a new trial in 1972 which took place in 1980 and found him guilty of manslaughter and sent him down for five years. He was released after a year and a half and determined to clear his name. The prosecutors in his trial were found to have hidden the testimony in a state investigator's document that pointed to Daughtrey as the most likely killer of Betty Renfroe. This document surfaced twelve years later.

Daughtrey, meanwhile, had moved to Ray City, Georgia in September 1971 and in the same month was charged with the assault of Jo Ann Peters at her Ray

City home. Her screams had brought her parents running and Daughtrey had fled. He avoided criminal charges and prosecution opting instead to go into the state hospital at Milledgeville where he was diagnosed as a 'hysterical neurotic,' I've not heard of that one before? He was released as 'cured' on April 19$^{th}$ 1972.

On August 3$^{rd}$ 1973, 27-year-old pregnant Emma Rogers was driving through Madison County, Florida on the Georgia side of the state line when her car was forced off the road and she was shot six times by a man who stole her purse. She managed to survive and gave the police a description of her attacker that fitted Daughtrey who was named as a suspect but not interviewed or charged at the time.

Four months later in Cook County, Georgia, Doris Register was chased in her car and forced to a stop off the road where she was shot in the head by a shot gun but survived and was able to give a good description of her assailant who had looked into the car and laughed as he shot her. She had also noted the registration number of his car. It was Earl Daughtrey's car. Forensics matched paint samples from Daughtrey's car with those on Register's car where he had forced her off the road.

He was convicted in Florida for the earlier attempted murder of Emma Rogers and given a life sentence plus fifteen years for robbery and aggravated assault with intent to kill. A second trial in Georgia added ten more years for the shooting and robbery of Doris Register to run consecutively. He served his time in Florida from September 1974 to February 1980 before being transferred to Georgia to serve a further three and a half years before being released by the parole board in June 1983 who said they 'honestly believed he had gotten his act together'. Hardly a ringing endorsement of him being cured.

On January 7th 1984 police were called to a public park in Tift County, Georgia where Daughtrey was in the act of trying to strangle 34-year-old Brenda Dubruhal. After driving off and ramming two patrol cars in a chase he was arrested and charged with aggravated assault, reckless driving and evading arrest. His parole was revoked and he went back into prison until his final release on February 24th 1985.

On October 29th 1985, Cheryl Fletcher was found dead at her home in Ocilla, Georgia, near Tifton. She had been strangled with a lamp cord tied with double knots around her neck. The police believed the killer had answered an advert Cheryl had placed in the local paper advertising some 'items for sale'. None of the items were missing and the police had no further clues. A second 'items for sale' advert murder happened on March 12th 1987 when Beverly Kaster was killed in her home in Lenox, Georgia. She had been strangled with a blouse double-knotted around her neck.

A break in the case came two months later when Louise Spotanski advertised a pair of chairs for sale in the local paper and was phoned many times by a man keen to do the deal quickly. She had read about the other murders and alerted the police of her suspicions after inviting the 'buyer' to come round on May 13th 1987. The police arrived quickly to find Daughtrey already there and menacing Spotanski with a towel already wrapped around his fists. He gave the police a false name and address and was sentenced to thirty days for making false statements to the police. He was released from custody after a week. Enquiries into Daughtrey were made and his telephone record examined. It showed a call to Cheryl Fletcher was made by him just a week before her murder. The same method of killing by strangulation with a double knotted material linked the three cases and with the telephone call as a reason to suspect him the police were given a warrant to search his home. Nothing was found. The FBI's Behavioral Unit did a careful appraisal and analysis of Daughtrey and concluded that he was the killer in all three cases and exhibited the traits and tendencies of a serial killer. But no solid evidence was held that would warrant an arrest and trial.

Elsewhere, in December 1987, Harvey Renfroe filed a suit against Daughtrey for wrongful arrest for the death of Betty Renfroe and claimed $32.5 million in punitive damages. Daughtrey counter sued in January 1988 denouncing Renfroe's suit as 'frivolous harassement'. Both suits were awaiting listing when Early Lewellyn Daughtrey Jr. died in 2008 and both were dropped.

# MARK ANTHONY DUKE

Born 1981 – sentenced to death in 1999, commuted to life in prison 2005.

This is a horrendous family crime that took place in Shelby County, Alabama.

Mark Duke, age 16, was angry that his father Randy Duke, 39, had refused to lend him his truck and on March 23$^{rd}$ 1997 went to the house with three friends, Brandon Samra, Michael Ellison and David Collums intending to kill the whole family and make it appear to be a robbery. Duke and Samra went inside whilst the other two waited in a car outside.

Duke shot and killed both his father and his father's fiancé Dedra Hunt, 29, before he and Samra searched for and found Ms Hunt's two daughters, Chelisa 6 and Chelsea 7 years old, both were frightened and hiding in the house. They cut both the young girl's throats. They then ransacked the house to resemble a robbery. All four then went off to a local cinema to watch the movie Scream, to establish an alibi.

The alibi didn't work and all four were arrested and tried for the murders. Ellison and Collums were convicted but as they did not enter the house they received long prison sentences of 16 years as accessories to murder. Samra and Duke both received the death penalty. Even though he testified against Duke, Brandon Samra was given the death sentence. In 2005 the U.S. Supreme Court made a decision not to execute 16 and 17 year olds. As Duke was 16 at the time of the murders his death sentence was commuted to life in prison. Brandon Samra was 19 at the time of the murders and wasn't so lucky. He was executed age 41 after 22 years on Death Row as his appeals wound their way slowly through the American judicial system until his defence lawyers were turned down finally by the U.S. Supreme Court and the sentence was carried out on 16$^{th}$ May 2019.

Mark Anthony Duke remains in a state prison in Atmore. Unless you know differently?

# HORACE FRANKLIN DUNKINS Jr.

Born 25th February 1961 – executed by electrocution July 14th, 1989.

Horace Dunkins was convicted of the rape and murder of 26 year old mother of four, Lynn McCurry, on 26th May 1980 in Warrior, Alabama together with an accomplice. The victim was discovered tied to a tree behind her home with 67 stab wounds in her body. Dunkin's accomplice was given a life sentence and Dunkins had two appeals turned down by the Supreme Court. These appeals rested on his defence attorney's claim that Dunkin's low mental ability had not been considered by the court or jury when passing the death penalty although the law requires this information to be given. He had an I.Q. of 69 which bordered on retardation. When this was made known long after the trial and execution several of the jurors made it known they would have passed a life sentence rather than a death penalty if they had been aware of his low mental ability. It led to a long debate on the rights of executing the retarded with most states taking for the life in prison option.

To compound Dunkins last hours his actual execution descended into farce when the first throw of the electrical switch at 12.08 on the morning of July 14th 1989 failed to kill him. The cable connections were not properly connected and the power had to be cut whilst officials re-connected them for the switch to be thrown a second time at 12.17. Alabama Prison Commissioner Morris Thigpen apologised for the 'human error'. Dunkin's head was covered by a black hood during this episode and it is not known whether he was aware of what was happening or had felt anything from the first throw of the switch.

Further later revelations emerged that Dunkins had not been offered a lawyer whilst being originally questioned at the Jefferson County Courthouse although he had asked for one, and that he later signed a confession without a lawyer or witness in attendance. Both revelations could have sunk the prosecution's case had they been known to the defence.

# DAVID RAY DUREN

Born August 28th 1962 – executed by electrocution January 7th 2000.

On October 20th 1983, David Duren, 21, and his friend Richard Kinder were out in woodland near Trussville, Jefferson County shooting with a pistol. They came upon 17 year old Charles Leonard and his 16 year old girlfriend Kathleen Bedsole parked up in a secluded area and after threatening them with the pistol ordered them out of the car before tying them together with rope and forcing them into the car's boot. Duren and Kinder drove aimlessly around for two hours and then pulled into a quiet spot and ordered the captives out of the car. Duren then shot Kathleen from close range hitting her in the head. She fell to the ground pulling Leonard down with her. Duran calmly stood over them and fired shots into Leonard's legs, hip and chest. Thinking they had killed both teenagers Duran and Kinder drove away. Leonard was still alive and managed to extricate himself from the rope and made it to a house nearby to raise the alarm.

Duran and kinder were seen in the car shortly after in Huffman, Alabama and arrested. Leonard identified both and identified Duran as the one who had shot himself and killed Kathleen Bledsoe.

Duran was remanded in custody on suspicion of murder and soon confessed taking police to the crime scene and recovering the pistol that he had hidden nearby. Both he and Kinder were sent to trial, Duran for murder and Kinder for assisting in murder. Duran was accused separately for stealing $40 from Bledsoe.

Kinder was given a life sentence without parole and Duran a death sentence.

Duran's appeals wound their way through the justice system at the same time as the U.S. Supreme Court was discussing whether Florida's use of the electric chair was a cruel and unusual punishment. It decided it wasn't and Duran was the first inmate on death row to be electrocuted since that decision. He had committed the murder aged 21 and was sent to the chair age 37.

During his time in prison he became a 'born again Christian' and was baptized in 1986. He wrote about his own crime and religious conversion which he posted on the internet calling it *'An Attitude Adjustment'* and recounting his self hatred at the killing of Kathleen Bledsoe.

Charles Leonard became a Baptist minister in South Carolina and had spoken by phone to Duran a few days before Duran's execution. He declined to talk about the call.

*A Letter From Death Row*

*Dear Friend,*

*Hi. My name is David Duren. I'd like to share something of great importance with you, in the hopes that my regrettable story will aid you in making some of the most important decisions in your life. First, let me tell you a little about myself. I'm a young, white male with an above average IQ of 132. I came from a middle-class family. As of 1988, I am currently on Alabama's death row awaiting execution.*

*Where Did I Go Wrong?*

*How did this happen?* That's an important question I've asked myself over and over again during the past few years. While waiting on death row, I have been able to accurately piece together the answer by reviewing my life. Why is the answer so important? If you will listen carefully with an open mind and heart to what I'm about to share, you can use my mistakes to check your life, and the lives of those you associate with, to help you correct and/or avoid making those same mistakes before they get too far out of hand. If your life is heading in the wrong direction, it can be corrected before it's too late.

*The Peril of Peer Pressure*

My real problem in growing up was peer pressure. I was a skinny little weakling, a "straight" kid, living in an apartment complex where nearly all of the kids lived with single parents, who had to work and leave their kids unattended. So, for company and fun, we all "hung out" together. I was not accepted, at first, by the other kids because I didn't do the things they did. I didn't curse, smoke, drink or smoke pot (marijuana). But I knew if I wanted to fit in, if I wanted any "real friends" (Ha!), I had to do all of those things. So, at age 12, I inhaled my first cigarette, drank my first beer, smoked my first joint of pot, and began to curse regularly. My peers said: "Aw, a little pot never hurt anybody!" and "Pot's not addictive -- it doesn't make you crazy!" I found out later that the medical experts say differently.

Guess what? It doesn't stop there! I've discovered by succumbing to peer pressure, I surrounded myself with so-called friends who drank, smoked, cursed and *did drugs. When you smoke pot, you've got to get it from someone who sells it. Frankly, I never met anybody who sold pot only. So, by smoking pot, you introduce yourself to the whole drug world. You also run the same risks by drinking alcohol. Suddenly, you need something to enhance your drink. So, you smoke a joint -- that's what I did. Then, you go buy your joint from your "connection," and he or she says, "Oh, man, I don't have any pot right now, but I've got some bad Quaaludes, or some crack, or a few Valium, Placidills, or even acid (LSD)."*

*The Dead-End Road*

*So, since you need a "high," you end up buying whatever is for sale. I should know, because that's the way it happened to me. Before you know it, you're not just smoking pot anymore -- you're crushing Quaaludes and mixing that with your pot. So, now you're all strung out and need a pick-me-up. Your friendly drug dealer says, "Hey! I've got some bad speed, man!" Or, "Hey! This cocaine will really put you in the clouds!" Now, you're flirting with death! What happens when you need a "fix" but can't pay for it? I think we all know the answer to that one. If you think you can do without it until you can pay for it, you're only kidding yourself. I was so bad off, I was doing heroin two or three times a week -- and I didn't even really like the "high"!*

*My favorite drug? Acid (LSD). I was doing it (even when I was in the Army) on the average of four or five times a week. I was doing it the night I murdered a 16-year-old girl (the reason I'm here now). Why? All because I succumbed to peer pressure! That's where it all started. It's been said, "Your friends can make you or* break you." Only later down the road did it lead to addiction.

Listen to Me!

I'm not writing this just to have something to do! I could be doing something else more pleasant. Do you think it's "fun" for me to sit here and tell you that I murdered a 16-year-old girl because I was so strung out on drugs and booze that I didn't know how to act like a responsible citizen? Do you think that's fun for me? No, it's humiliating, embarrassing, and generally downright painful to have to relate to someone.

Please, Learn from my Mistake!

So, I'm not doing this for me -- I'm doing this for you because I care! I don't want to see others ruin their lives and the lives of innocent people as I have. I've traveled that road you or someone you know may be on right now. That road is dark. That road is a dead-end street. I have reached its end. Its end is ugly. Its end is pain. Its end is lonely. Its end is death.

Have you or anyone you know ever witnessed a prison execution of death in the electric chair? If perhaps you could find someone who has witnessed an execution by electrocution, ask him to describe the sight of a man strapped into the electric chair when 1,600+ volts of electricity pass through his body -- the straining and creaking of the leather restraining straps. Ask him to describe the sight and smell of that man's burning flesh as the electrode gets so hot it sears like a branding iron branding cattle. Ask him to describe the sight of the horrifying mask that once was that man's face. It now looks like a macabre Halloween mask -- eyes bulging, face grimacing, mouth opened in a silent scream (not *because he wouldn't scream, but because the pain is so intense that he couldn't scream).*

*Maybe you realize the perils of peer pressure and are not into the drug scene. Good! You're on the right track. Maybe you know someone you care about who is now walking that dead-end street. If so, share this (letter) with them. Maybe you're hanging out with the wrong crowd that is influencing you to go places and do things you know you ought not do. I have cost an innocent girl her life, and I have ruined, I'm sorry to say, countless other lives by doing so. Please, learn from my mistake! I sincerely hope that what I have shared with you today is responsible someday for saving lives.*

*I am in the most awfully realistic, life-threatening situation, and my only hope is the salvation of our Lord Jesus Christ. While on death row, I ask for your prayers. Praise God, I have since been baptized into Christ for the remission of my sins (Galatians 3:26-27), based on my faith in Him (Mark 16:16), repentance of my past sins (Acts 2:38) and confession that He is the Son of God (Matthew 16:16-17; Romans 10:9-10). May the love and peace of our Lord Jesus Christ keep you.*

*In Christian love, David Duren*

# JOHN LOUIS EVANS 111

Born January 4th, 1950 – executed April 22nd 1983 by electrocution.

Another execution that didn't go to plan.

John Evans and his friend and fellow convict Wayne Ritter were paroled from an Indiana prison in 1976 and went on a criminal journey through seven states committing 30 armed robberies, nine kidnappings and two money extortions.

On 5th January 1977 they were in Mobile, Alabama and decided to rob a pawn shop. The owner, Edward Nassar, fought back and Evans shot him dead in front of his two young daughters who were in the store at the time. On March 7th the FBI received a tip off as to where the two were and arrested them in Little Rock, Arkansas together with the proceeds of robberies, the pistol used to kill Edward Nassar and another pistol stolen from the pawn shop.

Evans made a full confession but the state prosecutor refused to accept it as under Alabama law a death penalty can only be given after a jury conviction. Evans was sent for trial in Mobile, Alabama on 26th April 1977 for first degree murder with the prosecution asking for the death penalty. Throughout the trial Evans remained aloof and admitted the crime stating he would do it again. He threatened to kill each of the jury if he was given a sentence that included parole before he died. It took under fifteen minutes for the jury to return a guilty verdict and thus the death penalty could be, and was, imposed.

The Alabama Court of Appeals and Alabama Supreme Court both confirmed the sentence as was required by Alabama State law and a date of April 6th 1979 was set for the execution. Various appeals were made by his mother on matters of law and court procedures until finally the State Supreme Court validated the execution to be carried out at Holman Prison, Alabama on April 22nd, which it was.

The execution descended into farce. The electric chair at Holman prison was old, having been made in the prison work shop by inmates in 1927. It was painted bright yellow and last used in 1965.

The description of Evan's final minutes was described as follows:

*'At 8.30pm the first jolt of 1900 volts passed through Mr Evans's body for thirty seconds. Sparks and flames erupted from the electrode fasted to Mr Evans's left leg. His body slammed against the straps holding him in the electric chair and his fists clenched permanently. The electrode had burst from the strap holding it in place. A large puff of greyish smoke and sparks poured out from under the hood covering Mr Evans's face. A stench of burnt flesh and clothing pervaded the witness room. Mr Evans was examined by two doctors and declared alive.*

*The faulty electrode on the left leg was refastened and at 8.30 pm a further thirty second jolt of electricity was given. The stench of burning flesh was nauseating. More smoke emanated from his left leg and from under the hood. The doctors conducted another examination and reported that Mr Evans was still alive and his heart beating. At 8.40pm a further 30 second long charge of electricity was given and at 8.44 pm the doctors pronounced him dead. The execution of John Evans took 14 minutes in total.'*

See also the later section on **Wayne Ritter**

# PERNELL FORD

Born 1965 – executed in Alabama June 2$^{nd}$ 2000.

On the evening of December 2$^{nd}$, 1983 Wayne Griffith went to the house of his 74 year old disabled mother, Willie Griffith and his 42 year old sister Linda at 417 Goodlett Street, Jacksonville, Alabama where he found their bodies on the kitchen floor. Both had multiple stab wounds to the torso, neck and head. The house had been ransacked with personal property missing as was their car a 1978 Chevrolet Caprice with the number plate 11B-9461.

The next day, Saturday 3$^{rd}$ December, Pernell Ford, 18, was stopped on interstate 55 for speeding in Springfield, Illinois and the car found to be listed as a stolen vehicle connected to a murder case. Pernell was carrying credit cards belonging to Linda Griffiths as well as a loaded .38 pistol that was later identified as the property of Linda Criffith. He had no personal identification or driver's licence. He was arrested with the officers noting his bloodstained clothing and various articles of the stolen property from Goodlett Street in the boot.

Under interrogation Ford admitted the robbery and murders stating that his intention on entering the property was one of simple robbery but he was discovered in the act and Linda Griffith had tried to prevent his escape so he stabbed her. Willie Griffith was then screaming so loudly that he stabbed her to 'quieten her down' before continuing the robbery and leaving in their vehicle.

Ford already had a mental past and from the age of six had been in institutions being prescribed anti-psychotic and anti-depressant drugs. He had a history of suicide attempts.

Ford was sent for trial on murder charges in 1984 and immediately dismissed his lawyers. Despite his previous mental episodes the court found him competent to conduct his own defence.

They may have regretted this when Ford stated his only defence was that God would attend the trial and bring the victims back to life in front of the jury. He was dressed in a white robe and claimed to be able to transport himself anywhere on earth. He claimed to have four hundred thousand loyal wives in other countries and to have millions of dollars in Swiss bank accounts which would support them and his many hundreds of children after he was executed. He would die and become the Holy Spirit sitting next to God who he had met before. The prosecution cited all these acts as just a way of trying to convince the jury he was mad and get them to call for clemency and a life sentence instead of the death penalty.

However the guilty verdict was given and the death penalty handed down. The case slowly made its way through the appeal courts with Ford periodically cancelling his appeals only to re-instate them later. This went on until Ford was 33 in 2000 and was electrocuted in Holman prison on June 2$^{nd}$ fifteen years after committing the murders.

# THOMAS JERRY FORTENBERRY

Born 14th February 1964 – executed on August 7th 2003 in Alabama.

On August 25th 1984 Thomas Fortenberry, 20, walked into a gas station at Atalla intending to rob it to pay off his gambling debts. The cashier at the gas station, Wilbur Nelson, tried to talk him out of the robbery and during their conversation customer Robert Payne and his wife Nancy entered and seeing what was happening raised the alarm. In the resulting fracas Fortenberry shot and killed both the Paynes, Wilbur Nelson and Ronald Guest, the station owner's son.

Four local men with criminal records were indicted on the evidence of a local juvenile who professed to have seen the killings. These men were never prosecuted after the juvenile was found to have a mental illness past and admitted lying. Then in March 1985 a .44 calibre magnum Blackhawk revolver was found on the bank of Black Creek in Alabama City with four empty cartridge cases still inside. The Birmingham crime forensic department examined the gun and determined that it was the one used in the Atalla gas station murders. The Etowah Sheriff's officers made enquiries and established that the gun was in Fortenberry's possession in the days before the killings with three people positively identifying it and him as the owner. On May 2nd four officers visited Fontenberry at his father's house where he was living and took him in custody to the local courthouse, read him his rights and questioned him. He was joined by his father and they were left to have a private conversation after which Fontenberry took the officers to the place on Black Creek where the gun had been previously found and stated he had dumped it there. First of all Fontenberry accused another person of the killings before finally signing a handwritten statement on May 3$^{rd}$ admitting his responsibility for the robbery and murders and was indicted under the Alabama Death Penalty Act for four counts of murder.

The case went to trial with Fontenberry denying he had committed the murders and stating that he had been out with a friend called Underwood that day. They had been drinking and called at the gas station for more beer where Underwood had committed the killings. The jury returned a guilty verdict with a recommendation of a death penalty. As is the law an appeal was immediately launched and dismissed and other appeals challenging the court procedures and witness testimonies were started by Fontenberry's lawyers.

Fontenberry spent 17 years on death row before exhausting the appeals and being executed by lethal injection at Holman Prison on August 7$^{th}$, 2003 aged 39.

# DARRELL B. GRAYSON

Born February 26$^{th}$ 1961 – executed by lethal injection in Alabama on July 26$^{th}$ 2007.

On Christmas Eve morning 1980 the body of 86 year old widow Annie Orr was found by her son in her home in Shelby County, Alabama. She had been badly beaten and repeatedly raped. A pillow case had been taped over her head which had caused death by asphyxiation. Property from the house was missing including Mrs Orr's jewellery. Even her wedding ring had been wrenched from her finger.

The police were quickly on the scene and found a trail of dropped playing cards leading from the crime scene to a known burglar's home close by. It was that of Victor Kennedy. Kennedy had been seen the previous evening in the company of Darrell Grayson who the police went looking for. They found him hiding in bushes near to his home and carrying Mrs Orr's wedding ring in his wallet plus other pieces of her property were found when they searched his home. He was wearing a blood stained shirt.

Both men were arrested and charged with murder. Both confessed. Grayson told the officers that the plan to rob Mrs Orr had been hatched earlier that evening in Kennedy's house where the two had played cards with two other men until the early hours when the other two had left. They had talked of Mrs Orr's perceived wealth and decided to rob her at gun point. Kennedy had a .38 calibre pistol which they took with them and walked to Mrs Orr's house gaining entry through a rear basement door. Grayson knew the layout of the house as he had done work for Mrs Orr in the past as a handyman and gardener. They found Mrs Orr asleep in her bed and attacked her as she slept. They taped the pillow case over her head and when they couldn't find any money they beat and threatened her firing two shots from the pistol into the wall and raped her before leaving.

At their trials both were found guilty and given the death penalty. Kennedy was executed by electric chair in Holman Prison, Atmore on August $6^{th}$ 1999 and Grayson, now 46, by lethal injection on July $26^{th}$, 2007, twenty seven years after the murder

The time difference between the two executions being down to the number of appeals their legal teams submitted, all being dismissed. Including the last one by Grayson's lawyers which was promoted by the Innocence Project, a New York based charity that argued that DNA testing, not available at the time in Alabama, could have proved his innocence and should be mandated for all Death Row inmates. The Alabama Supreme Court denied the appeal.

# PHILLIP D. HALLFORD

Born March 22$^{nd}$ 1947 - executed by lethal injection in Alabama on November 4$^{th}$ 2010.

Phillip Hallford was a paedophile who sexually abused his daughter Melinda from an early age. In 1987 aged 40 he became obsessively angry at Melinda's involvement with her boyfriend Eddie Shannon, both were just 15 at the time and Melinda was pregnant. Hallford threatened his daughter and had her arrange to meet Shannon on a water bridge over the Choctawahatchee river in an isolated area of Dale County on April 13$^{th}$ 1986 where he waited out of sight in his vehicle with Melinda and his fifteen year old step-son Sammy Robbins. When Shannon arrived he shot the boy three times in the head and threw the body off the bridge. Afterwards Hallford used the spent bullet casings to make a necklace which he insisted Melinda wore. The day after the shooting Hallford returned to the bridge with Sammy with a bucket of water and a brush to remove any blood from it. Later that day with Melinda and her younger stepbrother in tow he burned Shannon's wallet and again visited the bridge to make sure Shannon's body had not surfaced in the water below.

Shannon's badly decomposed body was discovered by two fishermen in the river on April 26$^{th}$ 1986. An autopsy was held and the three bullet holes in the skull were found as were the three bullets embedded inside the head.

Neighbours of Hallford gave testimony to the officers handling the case that they had heard Hallford threaten to kill Shannon if he came anywhere near to the Hallford house. This concentrated the investigation on Hallford and when they went to bring him in for questioning he was found to have left the district with Melinda. He was found using a false name in a motel and arrested on May 23$^{rd}$ 1986 in Escambia County, Florida and extradited to Alabama.

At his trial in 1987 Hallford conducted his own defence. He denied any knowledge of Shannon and listed a false alibi for the day of the shooting which quickly fell to pieces. He then tried to blame the murder on his stepson, Cecil Robbins and told the court both Melinda and Sammy had mental problems and couldn't be believed when they recounted the day of the killing to the court. The guilty verdict was returned by the jury with a recommendation for the death penalty which the judge duly handed down. As he had conducted his own defence the court appointed lawyers to handle the required appeal process and once again the case climbed the steps of the US legal system until all avenues of appeal were exhausted and 22 years later on 4$^{th}$ November 2010, Phillip D. Hallford, now 63, was executed by lethal injection at Holman Prison Alabama and pronounced dead at 6.26pm.

Melinda was by then married with three children and together with her stepbrothers and other family members expressed relief that the 'nightmare' had ended. She had been very open about her abuser and the incest he committed saying that bringing it into the public arena had cleansed her sole. Eddie Shannon's parents attended the execution but made no comment.

# HENRY FRANCIS HAYS.

Born 1955 – executed by electrocution in Alabama on June 6$^{th}$ 1997.

Henry Hays was a member of the Alabama branch of the Ku Klux Klan. In March 1981 he was told by the KKK national leaders to up the profile of the Klan in Alabama and to show its strength and increase its membership.

Hays and fellow member James Knowles abducted 19 year old African-American Michael Donald at random from a street in Mobile, beat him, stabbed him and strangled him before stringing his body up in a tree opposite his house.

The local police, many of them members of the KKK, did a brief examination of the case and concluded that Donald's murder was the result of a drug deal that went wrong and closed the case.

Public outrage and the Federal Attorney's anger, plus the involvement of Jesse Jackson, brought in the FBI to re-examine the case resulting in the arrest of Hays, 26, and Knowles, 27, two years later. Both were sent for trial and convicted of murder. Knowles, who had turned state witness and appeared for the prosecution accepted a plea bargain of life in prison for violating Donald's civil right. Hays was tried six months later and sentenced to death. The usual ladder of appeals began and it took until 1997, 16 years later, for the final appeal to Governor F. James Jr who refused to commute the sentence and sent Hays, now 42 years old, to the chair in Alabama's Holman prison. Hays's father,

Bernie, a local Klan leader, had also been arrested for complicity in the murder but died before his trial

    As a result of the killing Donald's mother, Beulah Mae Donald with the help of the Southern Poverty Law Centre, sued The United Klans of America in a civil law suit for the death of her son. An All-White jury found the Alabama Klan responsible for her son's lynching and ordered it to pay Mrs Donald 7 million dollars. The result was that the Klan had to hand over all its assets and property including its national headquarter building in Tuscaloosa, Alabama to Mrs Donald who sold it off for $55,000 and bought her family a nice house. The Klan in Alabama was ruined and never recovered.

# LARRY GENE HEATH

Born 1951- executed by electrocution in Alabama on 20$^{th}$ March 1992.

An example of how the double jeopardy law was side-stepped by State lines.

In 1981 Larry Heath hired Charles Owens and Gregory Lumpkin for $2,000 to kill his wife Rebecca, 21, who was entering the ninth month of her pregnancy. On the morning of August 31$^{st}$ he left his house in Russell County, Alabama to meet the two killers at a place on the Georgia border near to his home. He escorted the pair back to the house, gave them the keys to the house and his car and left on his own in his girlfriend's truck. Owens and Lumpkin entered the house and abducted Rebecca in the Heath's car. The vehicle was found later that day at the side of a road in Troup County, Georgia with Rebecca's dead body inside it. She had been killed by a single gunshot to the head. The Alabama and Georgia authorities formed a joint task force to investigate the murder and on September 4$^{th}$ arrested Larry Heath. Heath waived his rights to remain silent and to have a lawyer present and gave a full confession admitting he had arranged Rebecca's abduction and death. He was sent to trial in Georgia and on February 10$^{th}$ 1982 pleaded guilty in exchange for a life sentence which could mean him serving as little as seven years. The trial was held in Georgia as the actual killing occurred in the State of Georgia. The State of Alabama was very unhappy at the leniency of the sentence and argued that the crime of kidnapping and murder had commenced in Alabama State and indicted him for the capital offence of murder during a kidnapping. Although Heath's lawyers argued his indictment unlawful under the double jeopardy law the court ruled in favour of the Alabama trial. During this trial evidence came out about Heath's engagement to a local lady from a very wealthy family whilst still married to Rebecca. He had hoped to marry this lady by divorcing Rebecca but she had refused a divorce. He had also claimed on Rebecca's life insurance policy shortly after her death. On January 12th 1983 the Alabama jury convicted Heath of murder during kidnapping and recommended the death penalty.

The defence lawyers hooked into the double jeopardy law that prevented a person being charged twice for the same crime and argued it in appeals on Heath's behalf through the court system right up to the U.S. Supreme Court who rejected it in this case and ordered the death penalty to go ahead. Heath was executed in Alabama on March 20th 1992. Eleven years after Rebecca's murder.

Owens and Lumpkin were arrested and charged with Rebecca's murder. Lumpkin was convicted and given a life sentence and Owens was also convicted and sentenced to death which was later reversed on appeal and changed to a life sentence also.

# JERRY PAUL HENDERSON

Born December 8$^{th}$ 1946 – executed by lethal injection in Alabama on June 2$^{nd}$ 2005.

A family gun for hire.

Jerry Henderson's wife Martha was aware that her sister Judy was suffering ongoing physical abuse from her husband Jerry Haney who was also having an affair in public. So bad was the abuse that Judy and her children fled to the Henderson's home and she asked Martha to ask her husband, Jerry Henderson, to kill Haney and offered $3,000 for the deed to be done.

On New Year's Eve 1984 the Hendersons hatched a plan in order to carry out the killing. The threw a party at their house and during the festivities Jerry Henderson sneaked out and went to the Haney's home where he lured textile worker Haney outside to the front porch and shot him three times with a shot gun, the third shot directly into his face killing him. Henderson then returned to the party to underpin his alibi that he had been there all the time.

Police suspected Henderson after a local phone box near the Haney's was used within minutes of the shooting to call the Henderson's house. However the partygoers supplied a good solid alibi and so the police played a ruse on Henderson telling him that they would be taking his shotgun in for forensic tests to see if they could match it to the killing. This is not actually possible with a shotgun as a shotgun discharges hundreds of small pellets whilst rifles and pistol fire one bullet which maintains minute scratches that fit the inside of the barrel of the weapon that discharged it. However, Henderson was not aware of this and the day before the police were to pick up the shotgun he reported it as stolen from his truck by somebody who had smashed the passenger window. Examination of the truck showed the window was smashed out from the inside not in from outside which confirmed the officers suspicions of Henderson but they still had no real evidence.

That alibi fell apart three years later after a Henderson family tift. Martha Henderson went to the police and admitted that her sister had paid Jerry Henderson $3,000 to kill Jerry Haney. The police had her wear a wire and they recorded conversations between her and her husband where he admitted the murder.

Henderson was arrested and admitted the killing and was tried in 1987 and convicted of Haney's murder as was Judy Haney. Both received the death sentence with Judy Haney's sentence being commuted to life in prison without parole at a later appeal.

Henderson's case went through the Alabama State appellant courts with a series of appeals all of which were turned down and finally to the U.S. Supreme Court where it again failed. He was executed by lethal injection at Holman Prison, Alabama on June $2^{nd}$ 2005, twenty one years after the killing. He did not make a call for clemency to the Alabama Governor on his execution day as was the right of all death sentence prisoners. As far as I can find out Judy Haney is in Tutwiler Women's Prison serving her life sentence.

# DAVID KEVIN HOCKER

Born May 20th 1971 – executed by lethal injection in Alabama Sept 30th 2004.

David Hocker had a list of criminal offences that started aged 16 after he became hooked on an assortment of drugs. They included burglary, criminal mischief, possession of marijuana, theft of a firearm and theft of money.

On March 21st 1998 he was working for Jerry Robinson, 47, who owned a small construction business in Houston County, Alabama and was seen with Robinson in a truck at a building supply company in Dothan buying fencing materials. Sometime afterwards Hocker stabbed Robinson to death and dumped the building materials in a ditch with Robinson's body in Henry County. He then stole the truck, Robinson's ATM card and cash Robinson had on him and made several ATM withdrawals. He bought $400 of crack cocaine from a street dealer and dumped the truck after falsely believing the police were on his trail. He rented a motel room in Mobile and phoned the police to give himself in after concocting a false claim that Robinson had made sexual advances towards him and the stabbing had occurred as he fought Robinson off.

Character witnesses testified Robinson had no homosexual leanings and was a happily married man with two children. When Hocker took the officers to where he had dumped Robinson's body they found it had numerous trauma injuries caused by beating and stamping which Hocker denied were from him. Forensic science examination of his boots disproved that.

Sent to trial for the murder of Jerry Robinson, Hocker pleaded guilty and was sentenced to death. The standard initial appeal was rejected by the Alabama Court of Criminal appeals and Hocker filed legal documents waiving his right to any further appeals. He was executed by lethal injection in Holman Prison, Alabama on 30$^{th}$ September 2004 aged 33, six years after the murder.

# WILLIAM JAMES HODGES.

Born 1960 – sentenced to death 2009. Sentence commuted in 2017.

Hodges is a suspected serial killer. His criminal career first came to light in 1999 when he was sent to prison for robbery after following an elderly woman home from a bank in Hamilton County and snatching her purse from her at her doorway. The Cincinnati police believe him guilty of dozens of similar purse snatchings, robberies and beatings of women from 1998 – 2003.

His first murder was that of 66 year old Winnie Johnson from Sumter County, Alabama who was shot dead during a robbery at her home on November 26$^{th}$, 2001. Later the same year on December 19$^{th}$ Hodges broke into the home of 58 year old Patricia Belanger in Pensacola, Florida, intent on robbery. When confronted by Belanger he beat her over the head with a claw hammer and stabbed her in the neck. During the attack two of Belanger's relatives pulled up outside the house to pick up Belanger for a pre-arranged trip to Idaho Falls. They got a good look at Hodges as he fled via a back window and they called the police who immediately started a major hunt. Despite a good description of the killer and his clothes it did not lead to Hodges being arrested. On March 19$^{th}$ 2003 in Cincinnati, Ohio, 81 year old Laverne Jansen was attacked, raped and beaten to death in her apartment. The police pieced together observations of witnesses that indicated she had purchased a lottery ticket locally and then been followed home. Once inside her apartment the killer had knocked at the door and forced his way in when she opened it. This was observed by a neighbour who had watched through her door peephole and had phoned the police. The police were slow to respond and took 16 minutes to arrive by which time Hodges had gone.

On September 5$^{th}$ 2003 Hodges was arrested for two attempted robberies in Pensacola and was remanded in jail to await trial. As a previously convicted criminal he was required to give his fingerprints and a DNA sample which were lodged with their respective Law Enforcement databases.

A cold case team had recently taken another look at the Belanger murder case and became interested in a photo found on her premises of a group of men, one of which was a known felon called Vonkish Golden, a cousin of Hodges. Golden was in prison and was interviewed. He told the officers that Hodges had been staying with him at the time of the Belanger murder and had worked on a relative's car the week before the killing. That relative lived next door to Patricia Berlanger. The officers compared Hodges recently obtained fingerprints with those from the murder scene and a fit was made as was his DNA and blood group. Hodges was arrested and charged. His story was that the prints and DNA were left when he went into Berlanger's to close her windows as he thought she had already left for her holiday trip and had left them open by mistake.

Further investigations in Alabama and Ohio resulted in Hodges being charged with the murders of

Johnson and Jansen in their respective jurisdictions. An agreement between them decided that Hodges, now 48, would be tried in February 2008 in Florida with the prosecution seeking the death penalty. He was found guilty and sentenced to death in February 2009. The appeals system resulted in his sentence being commuted to life in prison in March 2017 and he is still in prison in Lake City with the Alabama and Ohio judiciary yet to make up their minds whether to charge him with the other two murders.

# EDWARD DEAN HORSLEY Jr.

Born 1957 – executed in Alabama February 16$^{th}$ 1996.

See under **BRIAN KEITH BALDWIN**


# JAMES BARNEY HUBBARD

Born March 7$^{th}$ 1930 – executed by lethal injection in Alabama August 5$^{th}$, 2004.

This a fairly straightforward case of a murderer being executed for his/her crime other than James Hubbard, at 74 years old, is the oldest inmate to be executed in the USA.
In 1957 Hubbard was sent to prison for the second degree murder of David Dockery in Tuscaloosa County. He served 19 years before being released in October 1976. On his release he moved into the home of 62 year old shop owner Lillian Montgomery who was a Christian prison visitor and had befriended Hubbard during his incarceration and then sponsored his release.
On January 10$^{th}$ 1977 Hubbard called the police to Lillian's Tuscaloosa home saying she had committed suicide. Police found her dead with three gunshot wounds, one to the face, one to the head and one to the shoulder. A pretty hard thing to do, shoot yourself three times including twice to the head area? They arrested

Hubbard. They also found Hubbard had taken her gold ring, diamond watch and $500 in cash which were the shop's takings ready to be banked. Hubbard never admitted the crime and was sentenced to death.

The appeals process rambled on for 27 years with Hubbard hardly ever leaving his cell and not mixing with other inmates or taking any part in prison activities or exercising. Throughout the lengthy appeals procedures he maintained his innocence. Finally the Federal Appeals Court refused to block the execution as did the US Supreme Court and the Alabama State Governor was not asked for clemency.

James Barney Hubbard was executed at Holman prison on August $5^{th}$, 2004, twenty seven years after being sentenced.

# LARRY EUGENE HUTCHERSON

Born September 3rd, 1969 – executed by lethal injection in Alabama on October 26th, 2006.

On June 26th 1992, 89-year-old Irma Gray returned home from visiting a neighbour in Mobile, Alabama, to find Larry Hutcherson had broken in through the back window and was ransacking the place. Irma told him to leave and when he refused she tried to leave herself to get help but Hutcherson grabbed her in the kitchen, took a knife from the drawer and stabbed her. So vicious was the assault that Irma was very nearly decapitated. The medical examiner later testified that Irma's throat was cut ear to ear severing her windpipe and carotid artery, her nose was broken together with many other injuries giving evidence of a severe beating. She had also been sodomised. Hutcherson had left the house on the day of the murder only to return the next day and steal the air conditioner, microwave and other of Irma Gray's belongings that he could sell. For some reason he left his driver's licence and other personal belongings of his own at the scene.

A neighbour calling for a coffee with Irma the day after the murder found the scene and called the police. Hutcherson was quickly arrested and in his confession stated that on the day of the murder he had drunk a lot of beer and taken at least six valium tablets.

Hutcherson was sent to trial and convicted of the murder in 1993 and given the death penalty. His defence lodged a complaint that insufficient funds had been made available for the necessary experts to be hired to challenge the prosecution and the Alabama Supreme Court reversed the decision. He was sent to trial again on the same charges in 1996 and pleaded guilty to capital murder with the jury recommending the death sentence by an 11 – 1 vote. The case went through various appeals with his defence questioning various points of law and court procedures until the U.S. Supreme Court rejected his appeal and Hutcherson refused to ask the Alabama Governor for clemency as, according to his attorney, *'he doesn't want to beg.'*

Larry Hutcherson was executed by lethal injection at 6pm on October 26th, 2006 at Holman Prison. He had been on Death Row for 13 years. His extended family including daughter and sisters met with him the day of the execution but did not witness it.

His final words were for Irma Gray's family: *'I'm so very sorry for hurting you like this. It's been a long time coming. If I could go back in time and change things, I most certainly would. I hope this gives you closure and someday you find forgiveness for me.'*

# THOMAS TRESHAWN IVEY.

Born May 27$^{th}$ 1974 – executed by lethal injection May 8$^{th}$ 2009.

Thomas Ivey 19, who was being held in remand on a murder charge, escaped from Barbour County Jail in Clayton, Alabama with another inmate, Vincent Neuman in January 1993. They stole a truck and drove to Columbia, Neuman's home town where they kidnapped Robert Montgomery a local businessman and drove to Orangeburg County where Neuman testified later that Ivey shot Montgomery in the head killing him. Why he killed him is not known.

Two days later the pair stole another vehicle, went to a shopping mall in Orangeburg and tried to pass a cheque stolen from a cheque book left in the vehicle by the owner with his signature forged. The clerk of the store was worried about the near $300 spend on the cheque and said she would have to have it approved by the bank and alerted a staff security member who called the police and Sgt Tommy Harrison responded and let Ivey go when told it was Neuman who was the one trying to cash the cheque. As he walked away Ivey shot Harrison in the leg, later insisting the gun fired by mistake in his pocket and the bullet ricocheted off the mall floor into Harrison's leg. Forensics found evidence of this, the bullet was misshapen which it would have been had it hit the floor first and damage to the inside Ivey's pocket where he said he was holding the gun was also apparent. Ivey then shot the officer five more times as he lay on the ground. Ivey ran off pursued by several officers into the mall car park where he was arrested together with Neuman.

    Ivey was indicted for murder and tried. He was found guilty of Officer Harrison's murder by the jury who recommended the death penalty which was upheld by the judge. Neuman was sentenced to life in prison which he is serving in Carolina. Ivey's case was, of course, appealed through the court system until all appeals were exhausted and a stay of execution was denied by the U.S. Supreme Court an hour before he was executed by lethal injection at 6pm on May 8$^{th}$, 2009. Ivey was 35 at the time and declined to make a final statement. He was declared dead by the prison doctor at 6.15pm.

# ANTHONY KEITH JOHNSON

Born 1$^{st}$ June 1956 – executed by lethal injection in Alabama December 12$^{th}$, 2002.

This is a strange case. Why would a man be executed for murder when he didn't actually commit the crime and those that did have never been found?

On the evening of March 11$^{th}$ 1984, jewellery dealer Kenneth Cantrell and his wife were spending the evening at home in Hartselle, Alabama. Both had been in the jewellery business for near 25 years and had recently transferred it from a retail premises to be run from their home.

Mrs Cantrell took a phone call from a 'Bill Spears' from Florence, Alabama identifying himself as a jewellery buyer and asked to speak to Mr Cantrell. He told Mr Cantrell he was in the area and would like to buy some jewellery. They arranged for him to come to the house a short while later that evening. Something had bugged Kenneth Cantrell and he told his wife to hide his wallet and fetch him a .38 pistol he kept locked in a drawer.

A short while later there was a knock at the back door which led from the car port to the living and dining room of the house. Mrs Cantrel answered it and found it partly open with a man of about 45 standing outside. This man kept one hand behind his back as though concealing something and identified himself as Bill Spears. Mrs Cantrell asked what he was holding behind him and he replied 'nothing' and showed the hand. He then motioned another man that Mrs Cantrell had not seen, who was hiding in the car port, to come forward. He did so waving a gun at her as the first man grabbed her and said *'This is a holdup.'* Mrs Cantrell got away and ran into the living room where Kenneth was waiting and the man followed stooping behind a couch for cover as Kenneth raised his pistol and told him to *'freeze, I got you covered.'* The second man then came in and started shooting as did Kenneth Cantrell.

After a short period of sustained gunfire it went quiet and one of the intruders said, *'Come on in Bubba, we got him.'* As the two men walked back towards the door Kenneth Cantrell managed a final shot and Mrs Cantrell heard a cry of pain and then a scraping of boots on the car port concrete as though somebody was being dragged along. All went quiet and Mrs Cantrell called the police and an ambulance for her husband. Kenneth Cantrell had taken six bullets in the gun fire exchange with three hitting his chest and passing through the main arteries of his heart causing death.

The day after the murder on the evening of March 12th 1984, Anthony Johnson, 32, visited a friend in Newell, Alabama and told him he'd been shot in the back in a drugs related fight. He knew his friend had served in the military and asked if he knew a medic who could extricate the bullet. His friend did not and at Johnson's request drove him to a Motel in Newell, Alabama to meet Gene Loyd, another friend of Johnson, who asked where he had been to which Johnson said *he 'had to get the hell out of Hartselle.'* Asked why he told them he and some friends had gone into somewhere to steal some gold and got into a fight with security guards and he had *'got off a couple of rounds but taken one in the back. I think I got the son-of-a-bitch.'*

When his friend from Newell returned home he saw details about the Cantrell murder in the media and contacted the police. Johnson was arrested at the motel on March 14th, 1984 with the bullet still in his back. It was surgically removed and forensically matched to Kenneth Cantrell's .38 pistol.

This bullet was also found to have minute pieces of glass embedded in its nose. The glass matched that of the Cantrell's door to their car port which meant the bullet had passed through the glass before hitting Johnson as he was leaving the car port. Johnson was not identified by Mrs Cantrell as one of the two assailants in the house and could not have fired the shots that killed Kenneth Cantrell as he never entered the house.

Alabama law would not allow Johnson's testimony to be used to convict others in the case as he was a co-conspirator. At his trial Johnson was convicted of murder and the jury asked for a life sentence without parole. The judge refused their wish and sentenced Johnson to death. Perhaps this was because Johnson refused to accept a plea bargain of life for giving the names of his co-conspirators. No one else has ever been charged with Kenneth Cantrell's murder. It took 17 years for the case to pass though all the appeals structure before the U.S.Supreme Court upheld the death sentence and the State Governor refused a plea for clemency. Johnson, now age 46, was executed by lethal injection on December 12th 2002 at 6pm in Holman prison. He was the first to die in Alabama State's new lethal injection chamber after the state had disposed of using 'old yellow mama' the Death Row inmates name for the gaudy, bright yellow painted electric chair used previously. The lethal injection used three chemicals, sodium pentothal, Pavulon and potassium chloride to bring about death. The lethal injection chamber came at a cost to the State of Alabama of $185,000 after the state took the same line as many other states that the electric chair was inhumane and caused much pain. Two other lethal injection executions were booked to use the chamber before Johnson but both were granted a stay of execution.

# CHRISTOPHER THOMAS JOHNSON

Born 26th December 1972 - executed by lethal injection in Alabama on October 20th, 2011.

This is quite a disturbing case. On February 19th, 2005 Suzanne and Jason Mimms together with their young daughter Sophie spent the evening at the duplex of Christopher and Dana Johnson in Atmore, Alabama. They played board games, had few drinks and left at about 1.00am the next morning. At 9.00am Dana woke to find her husband and six month old son, Elias, asleep on the couch. Elias didn't respond to her touch and seemed totally limp. She noticed some bruises on him and couldn't find a pulse. She called 911.

The ambulance medics arrived and couldn't find any signs of life to Elias and performed CPR as they rushed him to the emergency room at Atmore Hospital. The medic in charge, Dr. Steven Sharp could not find any sign of life in Elias either but noted several bruises on the baby's face and nose plus ruptured blood vessels around his eyes and chin and a bite mark on one arm. Whilst inserting an endotracheal tube into Elias's throat to try and breathe life into him the medics noted blood in his mouth and stomach. Nothing worked to resuscitate the baby and Elias was pronounced dead. Because of the circumstances of the death the parents were taken separately to the local police station and questioned. Christopher stated that he thought he may have had something to do with his son's death. He said Elias had been crying during the night and wouldn't stop so he had laid on top of him to muffle the sound. When that didn't work he stuck fingers down the baby's throat and hit him. He thought that blow may have killed Elias.

An autopsy on the body of Elias revealed 85 separate injuries and multiple bruises. The medical examiner concluded that Elias's death had been caused by blunt force trauma and smothering.

Christopher Johnson was sent to trial on a murder charge in 2006 at Escambia County Court where he sacked his defence lawyers and conducted his own defence asking the judge to pass the death penalty on him for his actions. He told the court he intentionally murdered his son because he hated his wife and would have left her long ago if it was not for Elias. He killed the boy because he was afraid of the threats his wife had made of putting him in jail if he left her and did not keep up the alimony payments she would get from him for herself and the baby for many years to come. The jury found him guilty and he got his death wish when the judge handed down the death penalty. This was upheld by the Alabama Court of Criminal Appeals and Christopher Johnson waived his right to lodge any further appeals. He was executed, age 39 at Holman Prison, Alabama by lethal injection on October 20$^{th}$, 2011. His last words were, 'Game over.'

# AARON LEE JONES

Born 23$^{rd}$ April, 1952 – executed in Alabama by lethal injection May 3$^{rd}$, 2007.

On the 10$^{th}$ October 1978 Aaron Jones and his accomplice Arthur Giles broke into the farm house of Willene and Carl Nelson in the rural community of Rosa, Blount County, Alabama in the early hours of the morning. They intended to rob the house as Giles had worked on the Nelson farm and thought there would be rich pickings to be had from the wealthy Nelson family's belongings.

The eldest of the Nelson sons, Tony, 21, was sleeping in a bedroom with his brother, 10 year old Charlie. His 13 year old sister, Brenda, was in her parent's bedroom and their grandmother was sleeping by herself in another bedroom.

Tony was woken by a disturbance in the house at 3.27am. The light in his bedroom was turned on and showed Arthur Giles in the doorway. Tony's father appeared and ordered Giles to leave the house. Tony rose from his bed and followed Giles intent on making sure he left the house. As they stepped out into the yard Giles turned and shot him twice before re-entering the house. Tony's injuries to his chest and neck prevented him from following so he crawled under a nearby truck and in a short time heard Giles and another man leave the house. When they had gone Tony made his way back inside and found his sister and brother severely wounded. Both parents were dead.

Tony managed to get both siblings into a vehicle and drove to the local hospital where they received treatment for their wounds.

In his court testimony at Jones and Giles later trial Charlie Nelson testified that he saw Giles when his father asked Giles to leave the house. He then saw Giles and his brother, Tony, leave, heard two gun shots before Giles reappeared and shot his grandmother who was standing in a bedroom doorway, He saw Giles then go into his parent's bedroom and heard more shots. He ran into his parent's bedroom and saw Giles and Jones standing over them and his sister, all had been shot. He lay on top of his sister to protect her and saw both intruders stabbing his parents many times before turning and stabbing him and his sister.

Later autopsies showed Willene Nelson had multiple stab wounds to her heart, lungs and kidneys as well as numerous lacerations trauma from a blunt instrument as well as a gunshot wound to her shoulder. Carl Nelson died from a combination of gunshot wounds and stabbing as well as blunt instrument trauma.

Jones was interviewed on November 11$^{th}$ and made a confession to his participation in the events at the Nelson home that resulted in the deaths of Willene and Carl Nelson. He gave the reason for the robbery was that Giles had said Nelson owed him money for previous work he had done on the farm and not been paid for.

At trial Jones was found guilty of murder with the jury's recommendation of the death penalty being agreed by the judge who passed that sentence. The usual appeals followed with Johnson's defence listing various mitigating circumstances for his behaviour including an abusive childhood and drug and drink dependency. All the appeals were dismissed and Aaron Jones was put to death by lethal injection at Holman Prison, Alabama on May 3$^{rd}$, 2007, he spent twenty nine years on Death Row and was 55 when executed. Arthur Giles was tried separately and also given the death sentence. He died naturally aged 61 on September 30$^{th}$, 2020, after being on Death Row for 41 years and avoiding the lethal injection by using multiple time wasting appeals.

# ARTHUR LEE JONES

Born July 26th, 1938 – executed by electrocution in Alabama March 21st 1986.

At 12.45am on the morning of August 17th, 1981 Alabama taxi driver William Waymon, 71, was hired at the local taxi stand by Arthur Jones,43. The taxi company's dispatcher called Waymon to find out his destination but could not get a reply on the radio. Just half an hour later Waymon was found lying beside his taxi near to Jones's home in Plateau, North Mobile, Alabama. He had been shot dead and robbed. The taxi radio was working perfectly.

A murder enquiry was launched and an appeal for witnesses brought 'Shorty' Banks a local man forward who said he had seen a man hire the taxi and ask the driver to go to Plateau. Banks was shown a series of mug shots but couldn't pick out the man. For some reason a mug shot of Jones was not included in those photos? At a line-up three weeks later Banks did pick out Jones who he had described as fairly short. Jones was the shortest man in that line-up, a point made later at Jones murder trial when defence attorneys used this as the main defence tactic to ask for a miss-trial. This was refused. Jones denied the murder and two alibi witnesses were called who saw him at a social club at the time of the murder. Jones later claimed four other witnesses from the club were not called. The attorneys claimed to have contacted these witnesses who refused to testify. A man called Vaughan was named by Jones as being with him that night as they arranged a drug deal. The attorneys were unable to contact Vaughan in person but a man saying he was Vaughan did contact them by phone and verified Jones's claim but failed to appear at court to testify although he had promised so to do. The prosecution claimed Vaughan was a made up name and a ruse by Jones's associates. Vaughan was in fact a real person and is now dead so can't throw any light on the episode. The court found Jones guilty of murder in September 1982 and the immediate appeal was dismissed. As it moved quickly through the chain of appeals the remaining witnesses began to disappear and couldn't be found. Jones's last appeal centred on the fact that being a Muslim his faith decreed that he could not steal or kill anything and had been framed by the police was rejected by the U.S. Supreme Court on a 5-4 vote on March 20th 1986 as was a plea for clemency to the Governor of the State.

Arthur Lee Jones was executed by electric chair in Holman Prison, Alabama on March 21st 1986.

# ARTHUR JAMES JULIUS.

Born September 18th, 1946 – executed by electrocution in Alabama November 17th, 1989.

Arthur Julius had pleaded guilty to a murder charge in 1972 and was serving life in prison when, on January 29th 1978, he was allowed a one day release as part of his parole plan. He went to the home of his cousin Susie Sanders and raped and murdered her. Susie's body was discovered by her father and her daughter when they entered the house later that day and found her naked body on a couch. The furniture in the room had been knocked over and the telephone wire pulled from the wall. Forensic examinations found that the body was covered with bruises and 'rub burns' which indicated it had been dragged across the carpet. She had been strangled which was determined as the cause of death. Semen traces were present in her vagina, anus and mouth.

Suspicion immediately fell on Arthur Julius. His cousin, Willie Clayton, had collected him from the Draper Work Release Centre the morning of the murder at 11.30am and driven him to Montgomery, Alabama. Julius had asked him about Susie and whether she was still living at the same place. Later that day Clayton had lent his car to Julius at 3.30pm and it was returned at 6.30pm.

When Julius was sent for trial for Susie's murder two witnesses played an integral part in the prosecution's case. William Gray, a neighbour of Susie stated that he saw Clayton's car parked outside Susie's house at 5.15pm. Ruth Wheeler, Susie's second cousin called her on the telephone at about 4.00pm and Susie had told her she would call her back as her cousin 'Bobo' was visiting. Susie's mother testified that Susie always referred to Julius as 'Bobo'. When Julius returned Clayton's car, Clayton was with his brother-in-law, Orin Henderson, who testified that Julius had a fresh cut over his eye saying he had banged his head on the car door.

When the car was returned Clayton drove Julius back to the Draper Work Release Centre where Julius checked in with his Draper counsellor, Everett Rich, telling him that he was expecting a phone call as his female cousin had been robbed that day. Later he confirmed to Rich that he had taken the call and his cousin had been killed in the robbery. He said he had visited her earlier that day and all was well when he had left. Telephone records found no call to Julius had been recorded.

Susie's fiancé told police he had given her $30 when he left for work that day. He was a bus driver and took a bus from Montgomery to Meridan, Mississippi that day returning the following morning. His employer confirmed this. Records at Draper Centre showed Julius checked in $30 when he returned, money he did not have when he had left the Centre earlier. Forensic evidence found Susie's hair strands in Julius's underwear and material fibres from her house on his clothes.

Julius was found guilty at his trial and given the death sentence. His appeals were dismissed and on November 18th, 1989, eleven years after the crime, he was sent to the electric chair at Holman Prison,

Alabama. A last minute appeal to the Supreme Court to spare his life was dismissed by a 7-2 vote. He was 43 years old.

## VICTOR KENNEDY

Born 1962 – executed by electrocution in Alabama on August 6th, 1999.

See **DARRELL GRAYSON** section earlier in the book.

## ANDREW REID LACKEY

Born October 29th, 1983 - executed by lethal injection in Alabama July 25th, 2013.

On Halloween night 2005 Andrew Lackey was desperate for drugs money and broke into the home of 80 year old war veteran Charles Newman, a retired builder, in Hine Street, Athens, Alabama, under the false impression that Newman had a secret vault of gold bars. This had been told to Lackey by Newman's grandson who was a close friend. It was totally untrue. Once inside the property Lackey had been confronted by Newman who managed to call 911 and was heard by the operator talking to Lackey and telling him *'don't do that, leave me alone, what do you want?'* with Lackey repeatedly asking *'Where's the vault?'* Then there were gun shots heard. What the operator didn't know was that Newman had grabbed his own gun and shot Lackey who responded by stabbing Newman seizing his gun and shooting him in the chest, killing him.

Lackey then tried to drive himself to hospital but had to pull up and was arrested and taken to hospital by the police for medical treatment to his wound refusing to tell them how he got shot. He was quickly associated with the killing of Newman and his blood DNA matched to that found in Newman's house and on Newman's clothes. It was a cut and dried case and Lackey was found guilty of Newman's murder and sentenced to death. After the initial appeal Lackey wrote to the U.S. Supreme Court asking that no more appeals be allowed as he deserved his death sentence. He was executed by lethal injection at Holman Prison, Alabama on July 25th, 2013.

# MICHAEL JEFFREY LAND

Born May 23$^{rd}$, 1969 - executed by lethal injection in Alabama on August 12$^{th}$, 2010.

On May 19$^{th}$, 1992 a neighbour of Candace Brown, 30, noticed a window broken in her apartment and getting no reply he called the police. They broke in and found her two year old son unharmed and the family puppy, but no sign of Candace. A post-it note on a wall board had Michael Land's name and phone number written on it. A shoe print with a distinctive tread spelling out USA was found on a piece of the broken window pane. The telephone wires had also been cut. Candace had worked in the financial services sector and also part time as a prison ministry visitor advising inmates on their financial rights and budgeting. She had met Land briefly who was a friend of an inmate she was working with. Candace had suffered a previous burglary at her home just five days before when her purse had been stolen and she had told police of her suspicions that Land, 25, was responsible, but no evidence was found.

Police soon found Land at his work as a maintenance man in a local shopping mall in Hoover and he told them he had not seen Candace recently and provided an alibi for the day of the killing. His shoes were kept by the police after noticing the USA tread on them. Land's alibi did not stand up with the witness he mentioned who was unable to corroborate his statement. Land then changed his statement and said he met two men, Tony and Edward, at a service station and got into conversation with them whilst drinking beer. They asked him if he knew *'an easy mark'* for a burglary. He suggested Candace Brown's home and they gave him $20 to remove the window glass and they all entered the property later that night. Candace woke up during the burglary and afraid she would recognise him Land left the premises.

The following day Candace Brown's body was found dumped in a nearby limestone quarry near her home at Ruffner Mountain. She had been shot in the back of the head by a .45 calibre handgun. The bullet retrieved from her head matched that of a test bullet fired by police forensic scientists from a .45 calibre gun found in Land's car together with wire-cutters and gloves that had imbedded glass fragments consistent with the broken glass from Brown's window. A DNA profile from a semen stain on Brown's blouse matched Land's blood sample with a one in 20 million degree of certainty that it was his.

Land was charged and went to trial where the jury returned a guilty verdict and the death penalty was handed down by the judge. He was on Death Row for 16½ years before he was denied last minute appeals to the U.S. Supreme Court and the Alabama Supreme Court as well as the Alabama governor Bob Riley that his attorney lodged on his final day. He was executed at Holman Prison at 6pm on August 12$^{th}$, 2010 by lethal injection that was witnessed by Candace Brown's parents, her brothers and her son Michael, now 19 years old. Land had no final words.

# GERALD PATRICK LEWIS.

Born August 10$^{th}$, 1965 – died in prison July 25$^{th}$, 2009

Gerald Lewis had an unsettled childhood as his family moved between the Boston suburb of Brockton and Atlanta. His parents split when he was 11 and it was about then that he started a criminal career alongside any temporary jobs he managed to secure after leaving school at 16.

At 21 he was doing well with the proceeds from his robberies and sharing his life with a girl friend, Lena Santarpio. When she became pregnant her parents insisted she moved in with them and did not approve of her relationship with Lewis keeping him away from her as much as they could. The relationship petered out and Lewis disappeared until his arrest in 1998 for the murder of Kathleen Bracken. He then made a series of admissions.

Lewis admitted killing his first female victim in December 1986 after picking her up in Brockton and raping her, but he has not given enough details for the police to identify her. In 1987 he was wanted for the attempted murder of a five year old girl who was in an apartment that he entered to rob. He strangled her but her screams brought help and she survived when he ran off. His next known victim was Peggy Grimes from Georgia who was 8 months pregnant when she disappeared in 1993 and whose body was not found for five years. At this time Lewis was not a suspect and well below the radar of the police.

In April 1998 a 911 call about a murder in the Twilite Motel in Mobile, Alabama had officers racing to the scene where they found the body of prostitute Kathleen Bracken in her motel room. She had been stabbed and strangled with the later medical examination revealing sexual torture and rape.

The only clue to the killer was a man with a red pick-up truck being seen with Kathleen earlier that day. Enquiries with other prostitutes in the area revealed the man in the red pick-up was a regular customer and led to Gerald Lewis being a suspect. This was uprated to him being the killer when his DNA was found on a cigarette butt in Kathleen's rented room. After his arrest Lewis was very calm and confessed to Kathleen's murder and gave details of the other murders he claimed to have committed including Peggy Grimes, Misty McGugin in January 1998 and three other Georgia women.

Lewis pleaded guilty on counts of malice murder, criminal murder, aggravated violence, feticide and kidnapping with murderous intent. He was found guilty on the specimen charge of murdering Misty McGugin in 2003 and sentenced to death. Lewis died unexpectedly whilst his appeals were being heard on July 25th, 2009.

# MICHAEL LINDSAY

Born August 20$^{th}$ 1960 – executed by electrocution in Alabama May 26$^{th}$, 1989.

On December 14$^{th}$ 1981 Rosemary Rutland, 64, was stabbed and shot to death in her home in Mobile, Alabama. She was found dead by her relatives bound and gagged and with her home ransacked and Xmas presents she had bought for friends and relatives ripped open and stolen.

Michael Lindsay lived in a rented house directly behind Rosemary Rutland's and had done various pieces of work for her in the past. Police were notified that Rosemary's credit cards were being used at the local mall the day after the murder and set up a sting that netted Lindsay using the cards that he said he had found on the ground.

Lindsay was sent to trial for murder but the jury could not reach a decision and a miss-trial was declared. At the second trial Lindsay's wife and relatives stated that on the night of the murder Lindsay brought household items and Xmas presents into their house and made several trips to bring more. He refused to say where he was getting them from. These items were later identified as coming from Rosemary Rutland's home. Lindsay was also seen driving Rosemary's car on the night and his palm print was found on an item in her house. But as he had recently worked for her it was inconclusive evidence that he was the killer.

The main and most significant evidence against Lindsay was testimony given at the second trial by one of the officers who interviewed him that he had admitted the murder after his interview had been taped as they awaited transport back to his remand jail. The officer said Lindsay told him that he had killed Rosemary because she had recognised him. This was 'off the record' and the officer's word against Lindsay's. On record, just half an hour before that, Lindsay had told the officers that a man called 'Bob' he had met that day told him that he had robbed Rosemary Rutland's house and given him her credit cards and items from her house.

The jury at the second trial found Lindsay guilty of capital murder and recommended by 11 – 1 that the judge sentence him to life in prison. This jury was totally white, Lindsay was black. The judge ignored their recommendation citing that *'the crime far outweighed any mitigating factors,'* and handed down a death sentence. This was upheld on appeals right up to the U.S. Supreme Court and an appeal for clemency to the State Governor Guy Hunt was refused.

Michael Lindsay was sent to the electric chair at Holman Prison, Alabama on May 26th, 1989, 8 years after murdering Rosemary Rutland.

# LAM LUONG

Born 1970 – sentenced to death April 29$^{th}$, 2009. Conviction overturned on February 16$^{th}$, 2013.

Lam Luong made a meagre living as a shrimper off Bayou La Batre. After hurricane Katrina destroyed the area in 2005 he and his common-law wife, Kieu Phan, moved to Hinesville in Georgia where their relationship broke down. Phan, 23 at the time, moved herself and their four children to Mobile, Alabama after finding out that Luong was addicted to crack cocaine and having a relationship with another woman. Luong followed the family and unsuccessfully tried to find work in Alabama and repair the relationship but it didn't happen.

On the morning of January 7th, 2008 the pair had an argument and later that day, at 10am, Luong went to the local nail salon where Phan worked and asked for money. She gave him $31 which he spent on petrol for his van. Phan rang him later that day but got no answer until around 7pm when Luong contacted her and said he had left the children in the care of a woman called Kim who had absconded with them. Both Luong and Phan went to the local police station to report the children missing but once there Luong broke down and confessed to killing the children, Ryan, 3, Hannah, 2, Lindsey,1, and Danny just four months old. He told the officers that he had driven them to Dauphin Island and thrown them off Dauphin Island Bridge into the river eighty feet below. He took detectives to the exact spot.

A massive hunt for the children's bodies along the coast lines of Alabama, Mississippi and Louisiana was organised with anybody local having a boat taking place. It took two weeks to recover all four bodies. Autopsies showed all four were alive when thrown into the water. Luong was arrested and charged with five counts of capital murder, one for each of the children individually and one for them as a whole unit. He pleaded guilty and was sentenced to death in 2009 with an instruction from the judge that prison officers show Luong a picture of the children every day until his execution.

Medical and psychiatric tests on Luong following the sentencing showed he had an IQ of just 51 which was below that needed to meet the minimum required by the state and federal administrations for execution. Based on that the U.S.Supreme Court accepted his appeal and deemed it unconstitutional to execute him. The sentence was overturned on February 16$^{th}$, 2013 and he now serves a life sentence with no parole.

# DERRICK O'NEAL MASON

Born August 9$^{th}$ 1974 – executed by lethal injection in Alabama September 22$^{nd}$ 2011.

Angela Cagle was a 25year old shop assistant who worked the night shift in the Majik Mart store in Huntsville. At 3am on the 27$^{th}$ March 1994 Mason entered the store and held Angela at gun point forcing her into a back room telling her to turn off the CCTV camera which she could not do as never having been shown how to. He then had her take off her clothes and shot her in the face twice with his handgun. He then rifled the cash register and fled the shop.

At approximately 3.30am that morning Anna Lechman stopped at the nearby Circle K store to purchase some cigarettes. Circle K did not have the brand she wanted so she went to the Majik Mart. The South entrance was locked so she entered through the North door. Nobody was in the store and Lechman walked to the back storeroom to find the clerk. It was then she saw the nude body of Angela Cagle lying on the floor. Lechman rang the police from the store's phone. Forensic officers recovered Angela's clothing as well as a bullet from west wall of the storeroom and another from a shelf near her head. Black coat buttons were recovered near the body plus a negroid pubic hair entangled in forensic combings of Angela's public hair. Fibres of cloth that did not match any of Angela's clothing were found on her legs.

An unusual string of conversations with an unknown individual ensued when this individual phoned the police to ask the calibre of bullet used in the killing, a .380. The man made three calls in all, the last asking what make the gun was when told it was probably a Davis .380 the man agreed to meet the police and gave them the name of Derrick Mason as the killer. He said Mason was 'out of control' and out to make a name for himself in the criminal fraternity. The police checked on Mason and found he had an outstanding arrest warrant for assault and arrested him at a drive-through fast food outlet. A search of Mason's car revealed a Davis .380 pistol and five rounds of ammunition. Forensic Ballistics Experts matched the bullets fired from Mason's pistol in a test firing to those that killed Angela Cagle.

Derrick Mason confessed to the murder stating that he had wanted to get money to open a barber's shop. He stated that at some point in the storeroom Angela Cagle had attacked him and he had shot her. She fell over a table and he had shot her in the head as he didn't want her to identify him to the police.

Mason went to court and in 1998 was convicted of the Murder of Angela Cagle on a jury vote of 10 – 2 and sentenced to death as recommended by that jury. The conviction was upheld by the Alabama Court of Criminal Appeals in 1998 and the Alabama Supreme Court in 2000. Appeals were made and rejected by various courts until after spending 16 years on Death Row, Mason's final appeal for clemency to the Alabama Governor Robert Bentley was refused and he was executed by lethal injection at Holman Prison at 6pm on September 22$^{nd}$ 2011.

# MICHAEL KENNETH McLENDON

Born September 19$^{th}$, 1980 – committed suicide after shootout with police.

Something inside the mind of McLendon, 29, had been building up a hatred for his own family until it burst out in a shooting spree on March 10$^{th}$ 2009 and resulted in the murders of 11 people including himself.

He began his day of killing at his home in Kinston, Alabama where he shot his mother, 52, her three dogs and his girlfriend before setting the house on fire. From there he went to a relative's trailer in Samson, Geneva County in his Mitsubishi Eclipse and shot members of his family as well as a neighbour and her daughter inside the Big and Little Store in Samson. He then drove off stopping to kill a pedestrian at the side of the road before pulling in a petrol station and killing a customer in the shop. From there he drove along Alabama Highway 52 shooting at cars and killing a bystander who tried to stop him. The police were now on top of him and failed to stop his car as he drove into the yard of a Geneva company, Reliable Metal Products where he had once worked. He shot and killed a worker before engaging law enforcement officers in a gun battle injuring several including the Chief of Police. When the shooting stopped officers found McLendon's body. In just five hours McLendon had set fire to his home, killed five relatives and five members of the public and committed suicide.

It was obvious that he had planned this killing spree as he had armed himself with four guns – two assault rifles, a Soviet SKS and a Bushmaster, both with high capacity magazines which he had taped together, plus a shotgun and a .38 calibre pistol. During the spree he fired over 200 rounds of ammunition. His victims' ages ranged from 18 months to 74 years old. A note in a spiral notebook found in his belongings listed names of co-workers he thought had mocked him and places where he had worked and been sacked from. He also wrote that he felt his mother's family were not giving him support. It is hard to compile a list of places he worked at as there were many. He seemed unable to hold down a job for long. He had worked at Reliable Metal Products where he had been asked to leave. A reason for this was never given. He then applied to join the police academy and lasted just one week there before leaving. His last employment was at a Kelly Foods, sausage factory in 2007 where the company said he was a well liked team leader. He left a week before his killing spree. McLendon was buried at the Meadowlawn Cemetery, Enterprise, Coffee County, Alabama.

This was the deadliest spree shooting in Alabama's history. A local appeal for money to help the bereaved families with funeral costs raised $100,000 plus.

# WILLIE McNAIR

Born November 18$^{th}$ 1964 - executed by lethal injection in Alabama on May 14$^{th}$, 2009.

This was a straightforward robbery/murder case.

On May 21$^{st}$ 1990 Willie McNair and his friend Olin Grimsley had been doing cocaine and wanted to buy some more but had no money. They went to the home of Ella Foy Riley in Abbeville, an elderly 68year old widow who had previously hired McNair on many occasions to sweep and clean her yard. McNair asked her to lend him $20 but Riley told him she had no money. Mc Nair then asked for a glass of water and he and Grimsley followed Riley into the kitchen where he grabbed her from behind and stabbed her in the neck. Such was the force he used that the knife's blade broke off and remained in her neck. Grimsley took another knife from the kitchen cutlery drawer and McNair used it to stab Riley again. He then strangled her as she bled to death. McNair then took Riley's purse from the kitchen table and he and Grimsley left the house and dumped the purse nearby along a little used lane..

The next morning Riley's daughter found her mother's body. It didn't take the police long to list McNair as a suspect and he was hauled in for questioning the very next day. He admitted the killing and was arrested together with Grimsley. He took police to the spot where they had dumped Riley's purse and recovered it.

Mc Nair was sent for trial and convicted of capital murder in the course of a robbery on April 18$^{th}$, 1991 and sentenced to death by a 10-2 jury majority in favour. The Alabama Court of Appeals confirmed that sentence but sent the case for a new sentencing hearing after McNair's attorney pleaded that the sentencing judge had improperly considered a previous conviction of McNair's. The second jury recommended a life sentence without parole by an 8-4 vote. The court rejected this and again sentenced him to death. The case was twice more remanded for sentencing correction before the death sentence being finally affirmed. The U.S. Supreme Court upheld the sentence. McNair was executed by lethal injection on May 14th 2009 at Holman Prison, Alabama, 19 years after murdering Ella Foy Riley. Olin Grimsley is serving a life sentence without parole for first degree robbery.

# BRUCE D. MENDENHALL

Born April 14$^{th}$, 1951 – present day, serving two life sentences at the Turney Center Complex in Only, Tennessee

Bruce Mendenhall is a native of Albion, Illinois, a Vietnam War veteran, and led, what seemed to anybody knowing him, a normal life as a long distance truck driver. He married in 1981 and has two daughters. Friends remember him as a quiet man who even ran for mayor of Albion at one time.

The sharp eyes of a Detective investigating the murder of Sara Nicole Hulbert brought Mendenhall's serial killing of women to an end. The Detective noticed a truck on July 12$^{th}$, 2007 parked at the same truck stop on interstate 24 in Nashville Tennessee that matched the CCTV footage taken at the same truck stop on the night of Hulbert's murder. Inside the truck was a bag of blood stained clothing and other personal effects of a woman from Indianapolis who had been reported as missing the day before. Mendenhall was arrested and taken into custody. Further examination of the truck found 300 items, mainly women's clothing, which gave DNA samples of five different women.

Mendenhall mainly preyed on young prostitutes who were later found shot. When questioned Mendenhall admitted shooting Sara Hulbert whose body was found on June 26$^{th}$.2007 and shooting Symantha Winters, a known prostitute, whose body was found on June 6$^{th}$, 2007 in a rubbish bin at Lebanon, Tennessee. Mendenhall was sent to trial for Winters's murder, convicted and sentenced to life in prison.

Carma Purpura, 31, a mother of two was killed by Mendenhall on July 11th, 2007 at the Flying J truck stop on interstate 465. Her DNA, cell phone, ASTM card and some clothing she was wearing on the day she disappeared was found in his truck. Her remains were found four years later off the 1-65 in Kentucky.

On July 1st, 2007 the naked body of Greta Carter was found in a rubbish bin in Birmingham, Alabama with a plastic bag taped over her head. She had been shot with a .22 calibre weapon. Mendenhall was charged with her murder on July 28th.

Under questioning Mendenhall was initially co-operative and showed some sort of pride in his killings telling officers that he had killed six women at or near truck stops in Tennessee, Indiana, Georgia and Alabama, and then, probably under attorney advice, ceased that co-operation. Police are pretty convinced that other killings include;

Deborah Ann Glover, a prostitute whose body found on January 29th, 2007, near Motel 6 in Suwanee, Georgia. Mendenhall was in the area on the day of Glover's shooting.

Sherry Drinkard, a prostitute from Gary, Indiana. Found shot and nude in a snow pile.

Tammy Zywicki, a student found stabbed to death on September 1992 near LaSalle, Illinois after disappearing nine days before.

Robin Bishop, a prostitute who was run over at a Flying J truck stop on Interstate 40 in Fairview, Tennessee on July 1st, 2007.

Belinda Cartwright, a hitchhiker run over at a truck stop in Georgia in 2001. Witnesses produced a police sketch resembling Mendenhall.

In 2010 Mendenhall was convicted of the first degree murder of Sara Hulbert and sentenced to life in prison. Whilst on remand prior to the trial he offered money to two prison inmates, who were due to be released, to kill three witnesses who were going to testify against him. They told the warders about his offer and Mendenhall was further convicted of conspiracy to commit murder and had an additional thirty years added on to his sentence.

In 2018, Mendenhall was sent to trial and found guilty of first-degree murder in Tennessee for the murder of Samantha Winters and of connection to other murders in multiple states. This added another life sentence. In 2021 Mendenhall was transferred to Indiana to stand trial for the murder of Carma Purpura in 2007. The case is yet to be heard at the time of writing and he is in the Turney Center Complex in Only, Tennessee.

# ALAN EUGENE MILLER

Born January 20$^{th}$, 1965 – sentenced to death July 31$^{st}$, 2000

On Thursday August 5$^{th}$ 1999 Alan Miller left the house he shared with his mother in Billingsley and went to work as a delivery driver as usual. He had a job at Ferguson Enterprises, a heating and air-conditioning company.

But something was different with Miller that day. At Ferguson Enterprises he walked into the company with a gun in his hand and encountered Lee Holdbrooks, 32, another worker, and shot him repeatedly in the chest with a final shot to the head as Holdbrooks lay on the floor. Miller left the building as other workers arrived shooting dead Christopher Yancy, 28, on his way out.

Police arrived minutes after the first 911 call but Miller was gone. Another 911 call then came in from a gas company, Post Airgas Inc. five miles away from Ferguson Enterprises, also reporting a shooter. Police rushed there and found another victim, assistant manager 39 year old Terry Jarvis. By now a name had been given for the killer, Allan Eugene Miller, an ex worker. After a high speed car chase Miller's car was forced to stop and after a brief struggle he was taken into custody.

So what had set Miller on his shooting spree? It became apparent that he had issues with the men he had killed. At Ferguson Enterprises he thought he was getting the difficult deliveries and Holdbrook was getting the easy ones. Post Airgas had laid him off earlier that year when they downsized in the bad economic situation affecting businesses.

At his trial Miller pleaded innocent by reason of mental disease or defect although he had no history in that field. He was charged at Shelby County Court with all three murders and found guilty by the jury who recommended the death penalty.

After various appeals the U.S. Supreme Court refused to accept a final appeal and Miller, now 57, went to the death chamber at Holman Prison, Alabama to be executed by lethal injection on September 22$^{nd}$ 2022. Details of what went wrong are difficult to piece together but it seems because of his large size multiple attempts to access his veins failed and the execution was called off when the midnight deadline was met without success. Miller then claimed through his attorney that he had previously requested he be executed by the use of nitrogen hypoxia gas which had been approved in only 3 states, Alabama, Oklahoma and Mississippi and never used. Alabama denies he ever made such a request and states that the protocols for using the nitrogen gas were not complete and its legal use for executions is not on the statute book. At the time of writing Miller is back in Death Row awaiting judicial reviews of his sentence in Holman Prison.

# EVAN JAMES MILLER

Born November 2$^{nd}$, 1988 –sentenced to life in prison without parole on October 20$^{th}$ 2006.

Evan miller was just 14 years old when together with accomplice Colby Smith, 16, he attacked his neighbour Cole Cannon, 52, in his trailer in Alabama's Country Living Trailer Park in Speake killing him before setting the trailer on fire.

Miller's family lived in the next trailer to Cannon. Evan had been a problem child and at his subsequent trial for murder the jury heard from a defence psychologist that he was a troubled teenager with a drug dependency and personality disorders who had attempted suicide several times and had lived in foster care whilst in and out of psychological programmes several times.

It was just three weeks after Miller moved into the trailer that Cannon went to it on July 15$^{th}$ 2003 to use the phone to make some calls as his was out of order. Whilst making his calls Miller and Smith went to Cannon's trailer as they knew he had owned a Baseball Card shop and hoped to steal some valuable cards. They found a card collection and stole it plus $350 in cash. Cannon returned and caught them and a fight ensued during which Miller hit Cannon several times with a baseball bat knocking him unconscious. The pair then set fire to the trailer with Cannon inside and left him to die. The pair were not quickly arrested until Miller began to brag about his actions within his peer group a week later, and the police were told. He and Smith were then arrested and charged with murder. Colby Smith agreed to testify against Miller and to plead guilty to felony murder charges in exchange for a life sentence *with the possibility* of parole. Without that agreement he would have faced life without parole.

Miller went to trial and was convicted of the murder of Cannon and sentenced to life in prison *without parole.* The appeals ended on March 20$^{th}$ 2012 when the U.S. Supreme Court upheld the conviction. Miller has a history of crime and was first remanded aged just 14 and will never now taste freedom again. As the law stands, at the present time, all his life will be spent in jail.

# WALTER LEROY MOODY Jr.

Born March 24th, 1935 – 1997 executed by lethal injection April 2018 aged 83. The oldest person to be executed in the USA since the reinstatement of the death penalty in 1976.

On December 16th, 1989 Federal Appeals Judge Robert Vance opened a small parcel in his Alabama home which exploded killing him and seriously injuring his wife. Two days later Atlanta Attorney Robert Robertson opened a similar parcel which exploded killing him. Alerted by these events all mail to practitioners of the law and law offices was intercepted. Bombs were found sent to the Federal Courthouse in Atlanta and the NAACR office in Jacksonville. Both were diffused. By careful analysis the postal route of the parcels was plotted and a list of suspects known to be bomb makers was put together and details of the bombs' make up sent out to relevant departments. One bomb disposal unit officer recognised the similarity between the current bombs and one he had diffused nearly 17 years before. The name of that bomb maker was Walter Leroy Moody who had been convicted of being in possession of a bomb in 1972 after it had exploded in his house. He had served 4 years in prison.

Intensive police work eventually linked both the exploded and unexploded bombs to Moody who was put under surveillance. It transpired that in the 1972 case the rejection of appeals lodged by Moody against his sentence had started a festering hatred for the judiciary and justice system in his mind which had ended with the sending of the current 1989 bombs. Moody was tried in

1991 with testimony from the FBI, ATF, IRS, U.S.Marshalls and many others forming a solid case against him. He was found guilty of 70 different charges including the two murders and sentenced to seven terms of life in prison. A long series of appeals took place through the various courts until the US Supreme Court lifted a stay of execution and a bid for clemency from the State Governor was denied and on April 19$^{th}$ 2018 at 8.42pm, Moody aged 83 was executed by lethal injection in Holman Prison.

# DEVIN MOORE
# (Born DEVIN DARNELL THOMPSON)

Born May 15th, 1985 – currently (2023) on Death Row at Holman Prison, Alabama.

The carrying out of three acts of first-degree murder by Devin Moore sparked a worldwide controversy about the harmful effects of violent video games.

Moore killed two policemen and a dispatcher on June 7th 2003 after being arrested and taken into Fayette police station, Alabama, on a charge of Grand Theft Auto. Inside the building he told the officers *'life is just a video game'* seized one officer's .45 calibre gun and shot two officers and a dispatcher in the head killing them instantly. He then stole a police car and drove off. He was quickly apprehended in Mississippi and arrested on first degree murder charges.

Whilst awaiting his trial a TV programme '60 Mins' ran a segment where an avid video gamer compared Moore's crime to that shown in the video game called Grand Theft Auto: Vice City where a similar shooting occurs in a police station. The defence latched onto this and used it as a reason for Moore's behaviour with the judge discounting it and legal wrangles ensuing.

In August 2005 Moore went to trial and pleaded not guilty. He was found guilty and on October 9th 2005 sentenced to death by lethal injection. On February 17th 2012 the Alabama Court of Public Appeals upheld the conviction by a 5–0 decision. It will go at some time to the Alabama Supreme Court on appeal and if turned down can then go to the Supreme Court of the US. Moore awaits his fate on Death Row in Holman Prison, Alabama.

*Sidelines;*

Grand Theft Auto, known as GTA, is the most successful entertainment product ever made. The 11 main games in the series and its spin-offs are even bigger cultural behemoths than Star Wars, Fifty Shades of Grey or Lord of the Rings. The most recent in the series, GTA V, took more than $1 billion in its first three days of release. These earnings dwarf anything Hollywood can produce.

Unsurprisingly, the series has made multi-millionaires of its British-born architects, Sam and Dan Houser. Sam, 44, is president of Rockstar Games and the mastermind behind the GTA Empire. Educated at St Paul's School London and a graduate of both the universities of London and Cambridge, he has a reputation as a demanding perfectionist. He hides behind a cloak of anonymity and rarely, if ever, grants interviews. Brother Dan, 41, who also went to St Paul's before going to Oxford, is the writing genius behind the games, and vice-president of creativity at Rockstar.

The brother of one of the policemen killed and the parents of another are suing Moore, Rockstar and Sony as well as Wal-Mart and Gamestop who sold Moore the games. Moore's spree was not the first attributed to the GTA video game. In Oakland, California, detectives said the game provoked a street gang accused of robbing and killing six people. In

Newport, Tennessee, two teenagers told police the game was an influence when they shot at passing cars with a .22 calibre rifle, killing one person. But to date, not a single court case has acknowledged a link between virtual violence and the real thing.

# HUGH BION MORSE

Born January 1930 - April 2003 died in Minnesota Prison age 73.

Morse was a serial killer who travelled across the US in the 1950s and 60s pursuing his criminal career. Born in Kansa in January 1930 he was the product of a forced marriage after his mother became pregnant out of marriage. The marriage failed, the father disappeared and Morse had an awful childhood in the care of a brutal grandmother who despised both him and his mother.

Morse joined the Army in the 1940s and went AWOL in 1950. He was dishonourably discharged in December 1951 after being convicted of indecent exposure and assault in Wilmington, North Carolina in May 1951. He next came to the attention of the police when arrested in Los Angeles for a series of burglaries and served 6 months. In 1955 he sexually assaulted two 8 year old girls in an alleyway in Fairfield, was arrested and convicted being sent to California State Hospital for psychiatric assessment where he was declared a sexual psychopath and kept there until his release on probation in January 4$^{th}$ 1957.

Morse moved to Spokane, Washington where he got married, a marriage that broke down after just a few months, and he then began a peeping Tom episode in his life where he would secretly spy on women in their own homes. On November 7$^{th}$, 1959 he broke into the home of Glorie Brie, 28, and raped her before murdering her. Ten months later on September 26$^{th}$.

1960, he raped and murdered Blanche Boggs, 69, and then on October 25$^{th}$ continued the violent attacks by severely beating Beverly Myers, 23, in her home. She survived.

Three days after the Myers attack, on October 28$^{th}$, he travelled to Reseda, California where he broke into his ex-wife's home and attacked her with a knife. Unknown to him his mother-in-law was in another part of the house and her screaming caused him to run off and flee the State of Washington. A Federal Arrest Warrant was issued charging him with 'unlawful flight to avoid prosecution for burglary and attempted murder'.

Morse was now a wanted man and kept moving from state to state eventually stopping in Atlanta, Georgia where he broke into an apartment in April 1961 threatening the lady occupier and her three daughters. He sexually assaulted one daughter and left the apartment only to return to the same building a week later and entered another apartment where he raped an 18 year old girl at knifepoint. He then fled Georgia arriving a month later in Dayton, Ohio where he broke into an apartment in April 1961, raped and stabbed a woman several times before leaving her for dead. Miraculously she survived.

Fleeing the State of Ohio Morse went to Birmingham, Alabama and on July 11$^{th}$, 1961, broke into the home of Bobbi Ann Landini, 27 where he raped her and then murdered her by beating her to death with a lead pipe. In August 1961 the FBI was officially brought in to help locate Morse and added him to their ten most wanted list. In early spring 1961 in Atlanta,

Georgia, Morse raped at least two other women and was arrested on a separate charge of voyeurism there. He paid a $200 bail and walked away. He told officers later that he had been amused that a 'wanted' poster with his photo was on the wall above the counter where he paid the bail money and the officers failed to recognise him.

Morse kept on moving around state to state ending up in St Paul, Minnesota where, on September 18$^{th}$, 1961, he raped and murdered 34 year old Carol Ronan. The media increased their coverage of Morse and a few days later a member of the public recognised him from his newspaper photo and alerted the police. He was arrested on October 13$^{th}$, 1961 and told police he was relieved to have been arrested at last and admitted all four murders.

Morse was sent to trial in Minnesota on a specimen charge of second degree murder for the killing of Carol Ronan and sentenced to life in prison. In December 1963 he tried to commit suicide by slashing his wrists and neck in his cell but survived and made a full recovery. In 1979, now 49 years old, Morse was extradited to Washington and pleaded guilty to the murders of Glorie Brie and Blanche Boggs plus the assault on Beverly Myers. He was given life probation to be served concurrently with his murder sentence in Minnesota.

Morse died in prison in April 2003, age 73 and had served 42 years in prison.

# JOHN FORREST PARKER.

Born May 21$^{st}$ 1968 – executed by lethal injection in Alabama on June 10$^{th}$ 2010.

The Rev.Charles Sennett was a church minister who had money problems and was in deep debt. He offered Billy Williams, one of his tenants in a property he owned, $3000 to kill his wife, Dorlene. Dorlene was well insured so he would claim the insurance money and pay off his debts. Williams, in turn, offered John Parker, 19, and Kenneth Smith, $1000 each on 17$^{th}$ March 1988 to do the deed pocketing the remaining $1000 himself. He also gave Parker $100 upfront to buy a weapon. Parker used the $100 to buy drugs and had injected himself with Talwin, a pain killer, before he and Smith drove to the Sennett's Cherokee property on the18th March 1988 to do the deed.
Once there he told Dorlene Sennett that her husband had given them permission to look around the woods behind the property as a possible hunting site. They went off into the woods and returned later asking to use the bathroom to wash. Inside the bathroom Parker put a pair of cotton socks on his hands before coming out and grabbing Dorlene and beating her. He and Smith used a metal pipe on her and then stabbed her several times. They then smashed a medicine cabinet and took some items including a stereo and video player to make it look like a robbery gone wrong before leaving the property. They threw the stereo in a river and threw the knife into a pond at the property. Parker burnt all his clothes once he got home

When Charles Sennett arrived home later that day he found the house ransacked and his wife just about alive on the floor. She was taken by emergency ambulance to hospital but died of her wounds.

It didn't take long for the police forensics department to match hairs found on Dorlene's clothes and fingerprints left on the metal pipe to those of Parker's already held on record. The stolen Video was found at Smith's house.

The trial of Parker resulted in a 'guilty of capital murder' verdict with a jury recommendation of life in prison without parole. The judge overruled it and gave a death sentence. Out of the 35 US states that have the death penalty Alabama is one of just 3 that allow a Judge to overrule a jury. After the dismissal of appeals to the Alabama Supreme Court and the U.S. Supreme Court Parker was executed by lethal injection at Holman Prison on July 10$^{th}$ 2010, 22 years after the killing. Williams is serving life without parole and Smith is awaiting an execution date to be set.

Rev. Charles Sennett committed suicide a week after his wife's murder.

# EMANUEL BURL PATTERSON

Born 1979 – died in prison January 21$^{st}$, 2012.

On February 23$^{rd}$, 2003 at 6.30am a queue for work was already forming at the temporary employment agency building of Labour Ready Inc. at Huntsville, Alabama. The company describes itself as the nation's biggest supplier of temporary workers. Emanuel Patterson was in that queue and was a regular at the company looking for work. Something happened in the queue and an argument broke out over a CD player with Patterson being pushed around until something broke in his head and in a shouting rage of anger he pulled out a gun and started shooting. Three people were killed at the scene and a fourth died in surgery later.
Patterson fled the building, which was situated right next to a law enforcement office, and drove off. Police quickly identified the shooter as Patterson and got his address from the forms he had previously filled in when applying for jobs. They locked down his apartment and turned off the gas and electricity, it was a bitterly cold day and after eight hours Patterson gave himself up.
Patterson was charged with capital murder and attempted murder, both of which carry a possible death sentence.
There is little known or available as to the court hearings, if any, and Patterson died in prison on January 21$^{st}$, 2012. No details are available. If you have any please let me know so I can add them.

# MAX LANDON PAYNE

Born November 10th 1970 – executed by lethal injection in Alabama October 8th, 2009.

On March 23rd, 1992 Max Payne, 22, was at his sister Wilma's house in Culman County with his then girlfriend, Sandra Walker and Wilma. For some reason at about 8.30pm Payne took a double barrelled shotgun and went to West Point Grocery store owned by Baxton Brown and held it up. An alarm was set off by Braxton that alerted a private security company who called the police. When the police were alerted and attended the store it was empty.

Payne had robbed the store and kidnapped Braxton at gunpoint. He took the store owner to Wilma's house where the two girls were still at. They took $20 from Braxton who told Payne that if he were to take him back to the store *'I might just forget all about this.'* Payne refused the offer and took Braxton to a friend's house looking for .22 bullets. Why he was after these is not known as shotguns take cartridges not bullets. After he had left Wilma's house his other sister, Alma, went to the West Point Grocery store and told the police that Braxton was with her brother and the description of the car he was driving. Later that night the police found the car returned and inside were two spent shotgun cartridges and several unspent ones. Around midnight Payne bought a Greyhound Bus ticket to Florida using the name James Beavers. The clerk at the ticket booth noticed blood on Payne's jeans and cuts on his face and later was able to identify Payne as that man.

The next morning a partial dental plate was found on a bridge over Crooked Creek as well as blood stains on the bridge floor. A search found Braxton's body in the creek below. His face had been blasted off by two shotgun blasts.

When Payne got off the Florida bus at Miami he was met by detectives and taken into custody. A body search found Braxton's handgun as well as Braxton's driver's licence and car registration document, some West Point Grocery receipts, rings, food stamps, bank receipts and $1,085.84 in cash. Braxton's blood type was found in stains on Payne's clothing.

Payne was arrested and charged with three counts: 1) intentional murder committed during an abduction with intent to accomplish or aid the commission of robbery or flight there from. 2) Intentional murder during an abduction with intent to inflict serious physical injury. 3) Intentional murder during a robbery in the first degree in the course of committing a robbery.

At his trial an Alabama jury unanimously convicted Payne on all three counts and recommended a death sentence 11-1. The judge agreed and sentenced Payne to death. Payne was executed by lethal injection at Holman Prison, Alabama on October $8^{th}$, 2009 after spending 15 years on Death Row as his appeals went through the court system. No last minute appeals to the U.S. Supreme Court or to the State Governor for clemency were made.

# JOHN W. PEOPLES Jr.

Born January 9$^{th}$ 1957 – executed by lethal injection in Alabama September 22$^{nd}$, 2005.

Paul Franklin had a vintage 1968 Corvette car at his home in Pell City that John People's wanted to buy. He approached Franklin together with his cousin, Timothy Gooden, on July 6$^{th}$ 1983 and made an offer for the car but Franklin refused to sell. People's then killed Franklin and dumped his body in a nearby wood before returning to the house and taking Franklin's wife, Judy, and ten year old son, Paul, to the same spot and beating them to death with a rifle butt. Peoples and Gooden then made off with the car.

The family's disappearance was reported the next day by Judy Franklin's mother after the housemaid had called her to the house when she found it empty and the Corvette missing.

It would appear that Judy Franklin had concerns about Peoples when he was there as she had scrawled his name on a clothes hamper with an eyebrow pencil which the police found on July 10th. Peoples was already known to law enforcement for minor crimes and a hunt began for him and the Corvette. It took five days before he was caught after a call from drug store in Childersburg on July 11$^{th}$ about a man being a nuisance and trying to sell a Corvette car. The registration number matched Franklin's car and it and Peoples were taken into the local police station. It took two days before Peoples admitted to killing the Franklin family and took them to the place where the bodies were. All were in an advanced state of decomposition. All were blindfolded.

Peoples's cousin Timothy Gooden was implicated and arrested and immediately admitted being with Peoples on the day of the killings and agreed to testify against Peoples in return for a sentence of life without parole rather than the death penalty.

Peoples was sent for trial on three cases of capital murder and received the death sentence on each. It took 22 years for the appeals to be heard and dismissed until Peoples was executed by lethal injection at Holman Prison Alabama and pronounced dead at 6.27pm on September 22$^{nd}$, 2005 aged 48.

His final appeal was to argue that when he had been originally sentenced to death the electric chair was the death method. Alabama adopted the lethal injection method on July 1$^{st}$ 2002 and Peoples argued he had a right to request the chair not the injection. The U.S. Supreme Court ruled that he had missed the 2002 cut off date to request the chair and his appeal was without merit and therefore dismissed.

# EDDIE DUVALL POWELL

Born August 23$^{rd}$ 1969 – executed by lethal injection in Alabama on June 16$^{th}$ 2011.

In the early morning of March 25$^{th}$, 1995, Eddie Powell borrowed a friend's leather jacket and left the house he shared with Bobby Johnson, a co-worker at a local restaurant in Wesson, Holt, and crossed the road to rob the home of 70 year old Mattie Wesson who lived opposite. He was disturbed by Mattie during the robbery and brutally attacked, raped and sodomized her before shooting her and leaving her for dead and returning to his home.
Mattie wasn't dead and managed to stagger across the street to a neighbour telling her that she had been raped and shot by a black man. She then collapsed and died.
Powell was well known to the local police having been previously arrested many times for burglary and assault and was soon remanded into custody on suspicion of Mattie's murder.
He denied any knowledge of the killing but the forensic evidence told a different story. Powell's semen was found in Mattie's mouth, rectum and vagina. Her blood was found on his clothes and his handprint on the window sill of her house where entry had been made. After the murder he had given a handgun to a friend, Jason Long, asking him to get rid of it. Long could not recall where he had dumped it and It was never recovered. Items of jewellery belonging to Mattie were found on Powell. A matchbook from O'Charley's

Restaurant, where Powell worked, was found on the floor of Mattie's unfinished basement and had obviously been dropped there recently as it had no dust on it. Powell was also picked up on CCTV at a local gas station where he had bought wine paying for it with nickels and low denomination change. Mattie had a jar full of these, that she used in nickel and dime card games, which was missing. Her handgun was also missing and presumed to have been the one Powell shot her with and then given to Jason Long to get rid of. I would have thought Long would be charged with aiding and abetting a criminal act but can find no evidence of him being charged.

At trial Powell was found guilty of Mattie Wesson's murder and sentenced to death. He served 12 years and 9 months on Death Row until his appeals ran out and he was executed by lethal injection at Holman Prison, Alabama at 6pm on June 16th, 2011 aged 42, sixteen years, two months, three weeks and one day after the murder.

# HERBERT LEE RICHARDSON

Born February 16th, 1946 – executed by electrocution in Alabama on August 18th, 1989.

At 6.00am on August 16th, 1977 ten year old Rena Mae Collins and a friend had spent the night at her aunt Doris Wym's house and came out onto the porch to play. Lying on that porch was a bag with what seemed to be a drinks can inside. Rena picked it up and as she was about to throw it away it exploded killing her.

Police were made aware that Doris Wym had broken off a close relationship in May 1977 with a man called Herbert Richardson who had become a nuisance since by threatening and harassing her and the family. As the police looked into it the evidence stacked up against Richardson. The week previous to the bombing Richardson had thrown an object into the yard of the house from his car that had exploded. A threatening note had been put through the door on August 15th and he had been seen watching the house earlier on the day of the fatal explosion.

Richardson was an electrician and a week before the explosion he had shown two co-workers a bomb he had made and exploded it in a field. The police gained a search warrant and at his house found bomb making materials similar to those used in the fatal bomb and instruction books on Explosives and Bomb Disposal. He had also served for three years in Vietnam as an 'ordnance technician'. He explained that the bomb was just meant to scare the family and not to actually explode. A psychiatrist diagnosed him as suffering from

PTSD as a result of his military service and that would have contributed to his mind set and played a contributing role in his actions.

Richardson went to trial and was found guilty of capital murder and sentenced to death. On the day of execution, 18$^{th}$ August, 1989, the appeals ended when the U.S. Supreme Court refused to intervene following a decision by the Court Of Appeals in Atlanta which upheld a rejection of stay of execution made earlier in the day by a District judge. Richardson was executed at Holman Prison Alabama aged 43, twelve years after the killing.

# WAYNE EUGENE RITTER

Born January 30th, 1954 – Executed by electrocution in Alabama on August 28th, 1987'

See under **JOHN LOUIS EVANS**


# ERIC ROBERT RUDOLPH

Born September 19th, 1966 – sentenced to life in prison without parole August 24th, 2005.

Rudolph gained the nickname 'Olympic Park Bomber' after setting off a series of bombs in the Southern United States between 1996 and 1998 which killed 2 people and injured over 150 others. He is designated as a terrorist by the FBI and spent 5 years on their Ten Most Wanted list until he was caught in 2003.

Rudolph was born in Merritt Island, Florida on September 19th, 1966. His father died when he was just 15 and the family moved to Nantahala, Macon County, North Carolina. He did well in education and in 1987 enlisted in the U.S. Army. He was discharged in January 1989 for smoking marijuana whilst on duty having recently attended the Air Assault School at Fort Campbell in Kentucky.

The most notorious bombing committed by Rudolph has to be the bombing of the 1996 Summer Olympics at Centennial Olympic Park, Atlanta which killed spectator Alice Hawthorne and injured 110 others, many badly, with life changing injuries. In a later testimony Rudolph gave the reason for that bombing as *'to anger and embarrass the Washington Government in the eyes of the world for its abominable sanctioning of abortion on demand and to cause a cancellation of the Games'* It clearly failed in that as the organisers did not even cancel the remaining events scheduled on the day of the bombing.

Rudolph went on to bomb an abortion clinic in Sandy Springs, Atlanta January 16$^{th}$ 1997, the Otherside Lounge LBGT nightclub in Atlanta on February 12$^{th}$ 1997 and an abortion clinic in Birmingham, Alabama on January 29$^{th}$ 1998 killing police officer Robert Sanderson and critically injuring a nurse. The trade mark of Rudolph's bombs was dynamite surrounded by nails which acted as body piercing shrapnel.

Police first listed him as a suspect on February 14$^{th}$ 1998 after the Alabama bombing and then named him as wanted for the three Atlanta incidents on October 14$^{th}$ the same year. The FBI put him on their Ten Most Wanted list on May 5$^{th}$ 1998 with a reward of $1m. He went off the grid and spent 5 years as a fugitive in the Appalachian wilderness being hunted and seen at various times and places but not caught. He is thought to have had help from various Christian Identity groups and others during this time with internet groups praising him as a hero. Christian Identity is a white supremacist sect that believes that those who are not white Christians will go to Hell. They are also known as The Army of God.

Finally he was caught scavenging for food in a garbage bin behind a Save-A-Lot store in Murphy, N Carolina on May 31st, 2003. He was well dressed with new shoes and a trimmed beard which indicated he was being supported by friends. He was charged on October 4th, 2003 and on April 8th, 2005 the U.S. Justice department announced that he had agreed to plead guilty to avoid the death penalty with a condition that he led them to his 113kilogram stash of dynamite hidden in N Carolina, which he did.

He was sentenced on July 18th, 2005 to four consecutive life terms without parole and on August 22nd, 2005 a $2.3m fine was added and he was sent to ADX Florence maximum security jail as inmate 18282-058 where he spends 23 hours a day in his cell.

# GEORGE EVERETTE SIBLEY Jr & LYNDA LYON BLOCK

(I put this married couple together as that way the whole story works)

Sibley born September 8$^{th}$, 1942 - executed by lethal injection in Alabama on August 4$^{th}$, 2005.

Block born February 8$^{th}$, 1948 – executed by electrocution in Alabama on May 10$^{th}$, 2002

On October 4$^{th}$, 1993, Sibley, 50, and Lynda Block, 44, his common law wife, were fleeing from Orlando to avoid being sentenced for the burglary and stabbing of Block's former husband. Both had been very active in fringe political groups and had renounced their US citizenship some time before claiming the judicial system was biased and had no jurisdiction over them. They had destroyed all UD official papers that referred to them, their birth certificates, driving licences, insurance certificates etc.

Sibley was born and raised in South Bend, Indiana and moved to Orlando in 1976. A vehicle mechanic by trade he mainly worked on drag racers in his own workshop. He was active in political circles and libertarian issues. Block was a native of Orlando and a professional writer of news columns and short stories for several publications. She was active in community affairs and a Vice Chair of the Libertarian Party of Florida where she met Sibley. They published a magazine 'Liberatus' and married in 1992. Block had a son from a previous marriage.

They were in a car with Block's 9 year old son and stopped in a Walmart store parking lot for Block to make a phone call. Block left Sibley and the boy in the car.

Inside the store Opelika Police Officer Roger Motley had finished his lunch and was leaving when a lady approached him with concerns about a young boy in a car in the car park that appeared to being used to live in.

Motley approached the car and asked Sibley for his driver's licence. Sibley became flustered and Motley put his hand on his service revolver. Sibley then pulled out a gun and Motley moved quickly away to crouch beside his police cruiser. Coming out from the store Lynda Block saw what was happening, pulled a 9mm Glock pistol from her bag and fired at Motley hitting him in the chest. Motley managed to call a 'double zero', the code for help, on his radio as Block and Sibley kept firing at him. Motley died later that afternoon in hospital.

Both Sibley and Block conducted their own defence at their separate trials and refused to work with court-appointed defence lawyers. Both were found guilty of murder and sentenced to death. Both refused to lodge appeals stating that they did not recognise the U.S. Judicial system. Then, once Block was executed, on May 10th 2002, Sibley changed his mind and decided to pursue an appeal two days before his scheduled execution. It was dismissed and Sibley was executed by lethal injection in Alabama on August 4th, 2005.

Block wrote this in her cell as she awaited execution:

*"From Heaven to Hell," Written by Lynda Lyon.*

*It was fate - and a libertarian philosophy - that brought George and me together at a libertarian Party meeting in Orlando, Florida, 1991. George had been attending for a year when I entered the meetings for the first time. I was immediately at home with the small but active group of intellectual activists, and George and I were among a smaller group that together attended political rallies.*

*A year later, my marital problems came to a head and my husband agreed to leave the house to me and our son and to start divorce proceedings. At that time, needing to enlarge my fledgling publishing business, I accepted an investment partnership offer from George, who had seen my potential as a writer and publisher, and who had also seen an entrepreneurship opportunity for himself.*

*Our partnership, which had began as friendship, soon blossomed into romance - a true libertarian relationship of two highly intellectual, fiercely independent individualists who live passionately. We soon realized that we were soulmates - totally compatible in every way. We married in 1992 and our love and friendship has grown continually.*

*George helped me launch a new magazine - "Liberatus" -and we published hard-hitting articles about political corruption. We pioneered a revocation process that eliminated driver's licenses, school board surveillance on my home schooled son, IRS demands, and state revenue notices. Every document we filed was challenged by the various agencies, but after we sent them legal proof of our right to revocate, they went away. We taught others this process in papers, video, and seminars. We spoke on local talk radio. The local, state and federal agencies began to notice the influx of revocation documents from Florida.*

*Our hell began, not with the agencies, but with Karl, my ex-husband, who had decided to sue me for possession of the valuable house. He petitioned the judge to allow him back into my house until the case was settled, a preposterous idea. George urged me not to go to Karl's apartment to try to reason with him, knowing Karl to be a violent- tempered man. But I was desperate to keep my home and was prepared to offer him a deal, so George went with me. Karl let us in to talk, but he became angry at my attempt to bargain. In a rage, he lunged at me. George managed to pull him off, but Karl had sustained a cut from a small knife I had pulled out and held up as a warning just as he had grabbed me. The cut was not large or deep, and when we offered to take him to a medical center, he refused, though he did allow us to bandage the cut.*

*George and I were arrested in our home at 2:30 am that same night. Karl had called the police and told them we had broken in and attacked him. George and I had never been arrested before, never been in any trouble other than traffic tickets. We were in shock - George's face was pale and grim, and I felt faint when the deputy began to read us our "rights". They put us both, hand cuffed, in the back seat of a patrol car and we tried to console each other. We agreed not to make*

135

*any statements until we got a lawyer. I told him tearfully how sorry I was that he got pulled into this mess between Karl and me, and he assured me that it was all right, that he didn't blame me. I would have gladly borne the ordeal myself to spare him this. At the jail, as George was taken away, he looked back at me one last time and said "I love you, Lynda". Those words sustained me through the next five days of hell.*

*Because we were charged with "domestic violence", George and I could not make bond without a hearing, and we had to wait five days for that. I was placed in a cell with 30 other crying, arguing, loud talking women. I chose a top bunk on the far end, and sat and cried. I was terrified, because I had recently been interviewed on the radio about money being skimmed from the jail accounts, and the sheriff had ordered the radio station padlocked that night.*

*I could not eat those five days. The meat stank, and the vegetables and whipped potatoes were watery. I lived on whatever cartons of milk I could trade for my trays. I was astounded that the long timers would eagerly bid for my tray, and I managed to get paper and pencil as well. Writing helped me keep sane. I was able to converse with some of the women who recognized me as "fresh meat" and protected me from the lesbians and bullies. I called my mother to see how my son was doing, and she told me that Karl said he would make sure I went to prison and that he didn't want his son. When I began crying, the others stopped talking and looked at me. A large, black woman came over and hugged me to her ample bosom, and I felt a strange* kinship to these thrown-away, forgotten wives, daughters, mothers.

The most humiliating experience was the strip search. When ordered to strip for a body search, I froze. I had never undressed for anyone except my husband and doctor. Silent tears ran down my face as I disrobed, then turned to squat so they could see if I had any drugs protruding from my rectum. When I dressed, my face was red with shame. I felt violated, mentally raped. I never did get over that.

George and I did get out on bond the 5th day. We were sure that our ordeal was over and that we would soon prove our innocence at trial. We were so naive.

It soon became evident that politics had entered our case. Too late, we realized that our attorney had sold us out for a job with the county. When our trial date arrived, our attorney had done nothing - the witnesses had not been subpoenaed, nor records we needed. George and I immediately fired him and asked the judge for a continuance to prepare for trial. He said no - we either plead "Nolo contendre" or go to trial that day; and if we were convicted, we would be sent directly to prison for a mandatory 3-year term. Our attorney had an evil, satisfied look on his face and I knew we had been set up. We were forced to sign "No contest."

We were still determined to fight it; we had a month before sentencing. We filed papers exposing the corruption of the judge and the denial of our right to a fair trial, sending copies to the Governor, Lt. Governor, Chief Judge of Florida, Attorney General, and the Sheriff. Friends and supporters flooded these officials with faxes calling for an investigation, throwing their offices in an uproar according to a secretary in the Chief Judge's office.

We didn't show up for sentencing; we'd been tipped off that Judge Hauser was going to send us to prison anyway, under "orders." We had three days to file a temporary restraining order in federal court, but the man who had promised to draft the document never did, and a capias was issued for our arrest.

A friend in the Sheriffs department, and a member of my church, called me the evening of the third day, his voice shaking. "Lynda, the warrants for you and George came up on computer. I just heard there's a plan to raid your house. They know you have guns - they're going to use a SWAT team." I was incredulous. "A SWAT team!" His voice became softer, sadder. "You and George have made a lot of important people angry. They're going to kill you and then say you shot at them first. " He paused, to let this sink in, then said, "I've put myself at great risk telling you this. Please, get out of Florida. They mean business."

George had heard this on the speaker phone. His face was as somber as mine. As a last, desperate attempt to stop this insanity, I called to talk to Sheriff Beary. I had interviewed him when he ran for election. But he wouldn't come to the phone.

George and I were not criminals and we did not want to become fugitives. But my friend had made it clear we had no choice. At the invitation of a friend in Georgia to stay with him, we loaded our car and George, my son Gordon, and I left Florida that night.

The Shooting

*We stayed in Georgia for three weeks, but we knew we couldn't stay longer and endanger our friends. We decided to go to Mobile, Alabama, a large port where strangers come and go everyday, and figure out how to straighten out the Florida mess. We stayed in a motel in Opelika, Alabama while waiting for our friend to turn our remaining silver coin into cash, then we started out October 4, 1993, for Mobile. On the way I spotted a drugstore with a pay phone in front and suggested to George that we stop there so I could get a vitamin supplement and call a friend in Orlando. After Gordon and I came out of the store, he got back in the car to wait while George and I made the call.*

*While I was on the phone, George stood by, watching the traffic and people going by. He noticed one particular woman in a red Blazer pull in beside our car. She got out and looked at our car, a Mustang hatchback, with pillows stacked on top of all our belongings. It later came out at trial that she had presumed that we were transients, living out of our car, with a child obviously not in school. Actually, I always carried my own pillows when sleeping in motels. This woman's prejudicial presumption cost a police officer his life, my son his mother, and George and me our freedom.*

*Because I had run out of change for the phone, my call was cut off, so we left. But as we were leaving the shopping center I remembered my friend had an 800 number and I then spotted a phone in front of Wal-Mart. So George pulled the car into a parking space and he and Gordon stayed in the car while I walked to the store to call. Unknown to us, the woman saw a police officer* coming out of a nearby store. She approached him and told him that we were living out of our car and she was concerned about the child. She gave him a description of our car and left.

Roger Motley was the supply officer for the Opelika Police Department and hadn't been on patrol for years. He was irritated that he had to stop and check on this situation. He drove his car up and down the aisles, and when he found our car, he stopped behind it.

I had my back turned while talking on the phone and didn't see the officer pull up. When George saw the officer in the rear view mirror, he got out of the car, closed the door, and waited to see what the officer wanted. The officer approached George with the typical "I'm the guy with the badge and the gun" attitude. In a curt voice he demanded to see George's driver's license. George told him he didn't have one, and was prepared to get our legal exemption papers from the car. The officer then decided to arrest George and told him to put his hands on the car. George hesitated, knowing this was arrest, yet he had done nothing illegal. Motley, thoroughly irritated now, reached for his gun. When George saw him go for his gun, he reacted instinctively and drew his own gun. When Motley saw George's gun, he said "Oh shit'." and, with his hand still on his gun, turned and ran for cover behind the police car.

When I heard the popping noises, it took me a couple of seconds to realize it was gunfire. I heard people yelling and running to get out of the way. Quickly I turned and saw Motley crouched beside his car, shooting at George. Fear gripped my stomach. I *cried, "Oh God, no!" and dropping the phone, began running, ignoring the people scrambling for cover. I saw George standing between the rear of our car and the right side of the police car; he was holding his gun in his right hand, but his left arm was hanging strangely. Motley didn't see me approach, and just as I came to a stop I pulled my own gun and shot several times. He turned to me in surprise, and as he did, one of my bullets struck him in the chest and he fell backwards, almost losing his balance in his crouched position. His gun was pointed at me and I prayed he wouldn't shoot. Instead, he crawled into the car, and after grabbing the radio microphone, he drove off.*

*I immediately ran to our car and got in. The parking lot was quiet - everyone had sought shelter inside the stores. I was shaken, yet incredibly calm. "What happened?" I asked. George's face was extremely pale. "He tried to arrest me for not having a driver's license." He shook his head in disbelief. "I was going to show him our papers, but he didn't give me a chance - and he went for his gun." He looked at me, his eyes begging me to believe him. "I couldn't just stand there and let him shoot me."*

*I did believe him. George is the most honest person I know. He would not have placed himself or us in danger. He took the law seriously. He was never the show off gunslinger-type and would walk away before being drawn into a fight.*

*I told him that I believed him, but that we had just shot a cop and the whole police force would be gunning for us. We had to get out of there fast. It was then I noticed his arm and he raised it up to show me. With characteristic understatement, he said simply "I've been hit." His arm had been pierced by a bullet. Though blood was dribbling down his arm, it didn't obscure the hole. I examined his arm and could see that the bullet passed through his forearm and miraculously had not broken any bone or cut through a tendon or artery. I had an advanced medical kit in the car and I knew I could treat it later.*

*George manoeuvred our car deftly through the streets, trying to get us out of the area quickly while not attracting attention. I tried to calm Gordon, who was crying and shaking, and I looked at the map for the best route out. But we were unfamiliar with the area and kept running into heavy traffic. Then we picked up an unmarked police car and knew they were closing in on us. We were going over 100 mph when we suddenly came to a crossroad. We could only turn right or left. "Which way?" he asked. I was clueless - I had lost track of where we were. He took a guess and turned left.*

*We had gone only 1/4 mile down the country road when we came up on a rise - and then we saw the roadblock, at least 20 cars. George slowed down, then pulled the car over to the side of the road and cut the engine. He sat in calm resignation, then looked over at me. I said quietly, "I guess this is it, isn't it?" He nodded, then we both looked out at the policemen, detectives, deputies -coming at us from all directions, guns drawn, shouting "Get out of the car and put your hands up!"*

*It was an incredible, surrealistic scene, as though I was experiencing a virtual reality game where I could feel the action and motion, but then the game would end* and I would go back to living my real life again. My son's sobs brought me abruptly back to reality. I rolled down my window and put out my raised hand. "Stop!" I shouted. "I have a child in the car!" I could plainly see the closest officer's face turn pale, and he quickly spoke into the radio on his shoulder. "There's a child in the car!" he shouted. The Opelika police never told these Auburn police this. The word was quickly passed and then he said "Okay, ma'am, we won't shoot. You can let the child go."

I talked to Gordon, calmed him down, then I opened the door and let him out, told him to be a good boy and that they would take care of him, and pointed him toward a plain-clothes policeman. I gave him a last kiss, holding his handsome nine year-old face in my hand, to get a last picture in my mind of the child I may never see again. I watched him walk quickly away to the beckoning officer and I felt as though my heart would break. I had planned his conception, had nurtured him through sickness, homeschooled him. No one could have possibly loved a child as much as I loved mine, and he was walking out of my life only half-grown, unfinished.

As soon as Gordon was taken away, the police then shouted at us to surrender. I turned to George and asked "What do you want to do?" He had lost a lot of blood and was pale and tired. "I don't know." I made a decision for us. I told the officer, "We are not surrendering. You will have to kill us first."

For four hours George and I sat in the car and talked. I held my gun where the officers could see that we were not going to surrender peacefully. The officer continued to talk to me to get information about us.

George and I spent the time talking about the shooting, as he explained to me what happened. We discussed our plans for our future together, all gone. We discussed the probability that if the officer died, we'd be charged with capital murder and executed. If we decided to fight in court, it could take years. We knew we did not want to spend the rest of our lives in prison for an act of self-defense. We knew that it would be our word against a cops' word, and we had already seen how corrupt the justice system is. We then talked about suicide.

My religious belief is that suicide is wrong, but now I was faced with the total hopelessness of our situation. I told George that the only regret I had in all this is that I would not be able to raise my son. We discussed all our options.

As dusk settled in, we saw the SWAT team position themselves around us. The regular police had pulled back an hour earlier. A negotiator got on the police car hailer and tried to talk us into surrendering. We said no, that if they tried to come after us we would shoot ourselves. He then tried to bargain with us. What did we want? I printed my answers on notebook paper with a marker and George held it out his window for them to read - to talk to my son, to talk to the press, and to talk to clergy of my religion. He agreed to all these things (he lied - they did none of them), but we had to surrender first.

Finally, the showdown came. The SWAT teams had us surrounded. We were told that if we did not surrender in 5 minutes, they would lob tear gas through the windows of the car and take us anyway. George and I had been sitting with our guns in hand. We had *planned to shoot ourselves in the head at the same time. George looked at me with such sorrow and asked, "Would you mind if I stayed in the car and shot myself while you surrender? At least you could have some decision in Gordon's future."*

*I looked up at him with surprise, my eyes filling with tears at the thought that this honest, loving, gentle man who had waited over 40 years to find the right woman and found me, spending all those years in patient waiting, should now die alone with a bullet to his head. 'No," I said firmly, "I'm not going anywhere without you. Either we surrender together or we die together. I'll follow you, George - Whatever you want, I'm leaving it up to you." A totally surprised expression came to his direct, penetrating gaze. Until that very moment, he had not realized the depth of my love for him, that I would rather stay with him, even in death, and that I would trustingly place my life in his hands. "If we surrender, it will be years before this is resolved." "I know," I said, "but at least we'd be fighting this together."*

*He then took my left hand in his right, stained with blood where he had tried to staunch the wound, and raised my hand to his lips. "No," he said with renewed determination. "We will surrender so we can fight this. We have to do whatever we can to see that Gordon is taken care of, and to prove our innocence - if only for his sake." For the first time in months, hope was in his voice "We will fight this to the end, and it they still execute us, we'll die knowing we fought for what was right." He then gave a tired smile. "Yes," I said with respect and admiration for my husband.*

*With a look of tenderness I'll always remember, he leaned forward and kissed me, a gentle, parting kiss, perhaps the last we would ever share. Then, at a nod from him, we laid down our guns and exited the car with our hands up.*

The Trials

George and I were placed in solitary confinement in the Lee County jail in Opelika. The jail is small - the men's section holds 100 men, the women's section - 25. I was taken to a 4-cell unit in which I was the sole occupant. I was exhausted and numb - I had been fingerprinted, photographed, strip-searched and questioned. I had not eaten since breakfast and it was after 9:00 pm.

The cell block I was in was at the far end of the jail and hadn't been used for almost a year. After the last occupants had left, it had not been cleaned. One of the female officers pointed out a cell and told me to put my things there, then they left. But five minutes later they came back and took everything except the mattress, soap, toothpaste, and toilet paper. I stood there, dumbfounded. "Why are you doing this?" I asked. "Orders," was the curt reply and they locked me in the tiny cell.

George was treated similarly, locked in a cell by himself, but under the watchful eye of a surveillance camera. The bright fluorescent lights in our cells were not turned off for 10 days, and it was almost impossible to sleep. The constant temperature in the jail was 68 - degrees, and without, any covering, not even a sheet, I developed hypothermia, at times awakened by uncontrollable shivering. I would pace the cell to keep *warm but I was too exhausted to pace for long. George had no shoes or socks - they had taken those from him- and he too, was suffering from the cold. By the 6th day of constant cold I awoke to intense shivering, I was cold - inside as well as out; I was numb and could hardly move. With great difficulty I crawled to the bars of the cell and tried to raise myself, but couldn't. About 30 minutes later they found me on the cold cement floor, one hand grasping the bars, and they decided to give me a blanket. I wrapped myself in it and slept for 18 hours before my body temperature became normal.*

*I had to use my only pair of panties to wash myself and hung them to dry overnight to wear each day. They wouldn't let us shower, nor would they give us clean clothes. We asked repeatedly to use the phone to call our families so they could get lawyers for us, but they denied us that, too. The constant cold and bright light, the isolation, the starchy food - they all began to take its toll - as planned. We were both taken before Judge Harper for the initial appearance in handcuffs attached to belly-chains, and shackles on our bare ankles.*

*One cannot imagine the pain of trying to walk with shackles on your ankles, on bare skin. The proper procedure is to place them on the pants legs, but the jailers deliberately put them on our skin to inflict pain. George and I bore the pain without comment - we were not going to let them gain satisfaction from their torture. I still have scars on my ankles where the shackles dug deep into my skin.*

*At both court appearances the media was there in swarms. At the first appearance, Judge Harper - the* star - imperiously went through the routine of asking if we understood the charge - capital murder - and that the penalty was death or life without parole. Did we have lawyers or did we want the state to provide them? We both looked at him in disbelief. They all knew we had been denied even one phone call - how could we have retained lawyers? If George and I were not so exhausted and disheartened, we would have insisted on handling our own case. But they would not let us talk and discuss this. The prosecutor had quickly figured out from looking through my files and our legal papers that were in the car that we were well-educated, and politically and legally astute. He did not want us to handle our own case, thus the psychological torture to force us to take their lawyers.

After we were appointed lawyers, suddenly everything changed. They let us shower and use the phone. We received all our bedding and basic toiletries. We began to receive mail. Because George and I were so well known, the news of the shooting went all around the country, and calls and faxes to the Sheriff had come in asking about us. My mother had called and begged the Sheriff to let her talk to me but he curtly told her I was going to die for killing a cop and hung up on her. A friend had travelled all the way from Orlando to see what he could do for us and they refused him. Letters began pouring in, but we didn't get them. The prosecutor, judge and the Sheriff conspired to cut us off from all contact with support.

Despite the cruelties I suffered, none was worse than what they did to George. After they let us receive mail, a friend sent us stationary, pens and stamps. It was a long shot but I asked if George and I could exchange letters. Surprisingly, they said yes. (We found out later that the prosecutor had the jailers copy our letters for information.) When George wrote, he told me that the wound in his arm had been treated only once - at the hospital right after we surrendered. Over a week had gone by and they had not given him any antibiotics. Once, just before he was to appear in court, an officer put peroxide in his wound and changed his bandage. George wrote me that he could feel itching and could smell infection setting in.

As angry as I was of their treatment of me, I was more angry at their deliberate indifference to his obvious medical condition. We had just been given permission to use the phone and I called a friend and told him what they were doing to George. He immediately put out an urgent fax message to our supporters nationwide and we were told that the next day the Sheriff's office was swamped with faxes and phone calls demanding that George be properly treated immediately. Pat Sutton, a retired deputy, quoted law and Supreme Court decisions to the Sheriff about the proper treatment of prisoners. Early the next morning George was taken to a doctor who treated his wound and prescribed antibiotics. An officer later told George they had been given a prescription for antibiotics at the hospital, but the Sheriff would not authorize it to be filled.

From the moment we were introduced to our court-appointed lawyers, George and I fought to have them recognize that we were as knowledgeable of the Constitution and the law as they. We soon realized that we were more knowledgeable then they; all they knew was what they were spoon-fed at law school. They knew nothing about the common-law rights of self-defence, of the significance of the 14th Amendment citizenship, of the right to resist unlawful arrest. They refused to combine our cases, kept trying to put me against George so I would get a lighter sentence, kept repeating the phrase "We're doing this for appeal." We soon realized that they were not considering our innocence, but only the degree of our "guilt." They didn't expect acquittal, weren't working for it at all, and only wanted to work toward saving us from the electric chair.

George and I refused to submit to their plans - George's lead attorney tried to quit; mine left town and was replaced. George's attorneys did not prepare for trial. They had not sent the witness subpoenas out in time, so few came. They had not examined the forensic reports or questioned potential witnesses about the officer's violent nature. At trial, the prosecutor purposely twisted the facts in his closing statement to make it appear that it was George's bullet - not mine - that killed the officer. When George and I insisted that I testify to show that it wasn't George's bullet, George's attorney made the loudest protest. My attorney begged me not to testify. "George is already lost. Don't throw away your chance for life. Don't be a hero." I looked him straight in the eye. "I'm not doing this to be a hero. I'm doing it because it's the right thing to do."

I had prayed that I would be calm while I was on the stand, and I was. This, however, was interpreted by the media and the jury as "cold-blooded lack of remorse." During his trial, George was pale and tired, *and extremely thin. And he knew he was lost. It was inevitable that he would be convicted and sentenced to death.*

*When the jury recommended death for George, the jailers expected me to cry and wail. Because I showed no reaction and went about my normal routine, keeping my grief to myself, some of the jailers turned against me, convinced I was cold and heartless about George's plight. It was only after George had been taken away to prison three weeks later that I broke down. Clutching his last letter, written hurriedly just before they took him away, I cried quietly for hours. Half of me had been torn away and now I couldn't even hope for a glimpse of him in court, and receive his daily letters of love and encouragement. The reality of our situation only hit me then, when they took George away to Death Row.*

*I now had to concentrate on my own trial, which was getting nowhere. My lawyers and I argued at every meeting because they refused to even consider the Constitutional issues I knew were crucial to my case. One night I perpended the realization that unless these issues were raised at trial, I could not raise them in appeal - according to the ABA Rules of Court - and I would have no basis for a demand of my release. I had no choice but to fire these useless attorneys and conduct my own trial.*

*The next morning, at a closed-chamber session between the judge, my lawyers and me, I presented the lawyers their dismissals, and copies to the judge. Judge Harper only raised his eyebrows in surprise and ordered that the lawyers and I discuss this privately.*

*When we were alone, the lead attorney exploded in anger. "You arrogant fool. Why do you insist on throwing your life away! Do you have a death wish?" I was calm and even smiled a little. "You are not interested in proving me innocent - only of getting me a lighter sentence. I want acquittal or nothing. I may lose anyway, but at least it will be done my way." He stormed out angrily, and the other attorney shook his head in sympathy. "I know why you're doing this, but you're making a big mistake. You're risking your life." I nodded. "I know, but it is my life, isn't it?"*

*To prepare for trial in the 3 months I had, I read the Rules of Procedure and Rules of Evidence. I filed several pre-trial documents, unusual documents that I convinced the judge were to be introduced as evidence at trial. Fortunately, the judge was too ignorant of the documents and of Constitutional law to realize what I filed. Though he and the prosecutors scoffed at my pretrial documents challenging his jurisdiction, the Constitutionality of the statute I was charged under, and the validity of the indictment based on the original 13th Amendment; I knew that if I did lose, I still could raise this issue on appeal because it had been raised at trial.*

*The trial was a play, scripted by the judge, the prosecutor, and the restrictive ABA Rules of Procedure. In both our cases, Judge Harper refused to release the officer's personnel record, which showed a long pattern of abuse to the public, and I was working against a one-sided portrayal of the officer as a "good cop gunned down in cold blood." I was able to perform all the functions of trial in a calm, business-like manner, and even the judge grudgingly admitted how well I was conducting my defence. But under the restrictive rules of procedure in today's courts I had little chance, and I knew it. All I could hope to do was manoeuvre the trial to get as much information in my favour on record - for appeal.*

*When the jury came back with the guilty verdict I was not surprised, but it hit me hard. No one can possibly imagine being alone in a courtroom, feeling the eyes of everyone else upon you waiting for your reaction to the news that they were going to put you to death in a most horrible manner. I forced myself to sit perfectly still, emotionless, while realizing that the people of Alabama wanted to kill me for choosing to defend my husband's life.*

*When it came time for the sentencing portion of the trial, when I was supposed to convince the jury they should give me life without parole instead of the death penalty, I waived my time, telling everyone in that courtroom that I had presented everything I had at trial. I was not going to beg for my life. When I was awaiting their decision, I prayed that they would give me death. If George and I were both on Death Row, we could join our appeal and fight together. When the jury recommended death, I rose from the defence table with as much dignity as I could evoke and walked through the silent courtroom and hallways back to my cell. Some of the jailers were upset. One of the women in my cell broke down and cried.*

*Execution by electric chair is gruesome. They shave your head so they can attach the electrodes to bare skin. They shove cotton up your rectum and put an adult diaper on you because the charge of electricity through your body causes your bladder and intestines to evacuate. They put a hood over your face because the jolt of 20,000 volts causes your face to contort and your eyeballs to explode.*

*George and had agreed at the roadblock that we would fight to the end, and if we still lose and are executed, we will go back to our Creator knowing that we fought to the end, and fought for the principle that it is better to have fought and lost than to submit to those who would rob us of our unalienable right to liberty.*

# DANIEL LEE SIEBERT

Born June 17th, 1954 – convicted of manslaughter in 1979. Sentenced to death in Alabama on March 21st, 1987. Died from pancreatic cancer in Holman prison Alabama on April 22nd, 2008 aged 53.

Sherri Weathers was a hearing impaired student at the Alabama Institute for the Deaf and Blind at Talladega. On February 24th, 1986, after she had missed a week of classes her tutor phoned the manager of her apartment block concerned that she might be ill. The manager could get no reply at her door and used his pass key to enter Sherri's apartment where he found her dead along with her two small sons, five year old Chad and Joseph, four. The bodies were under a sheet on Sherri's bed.

The police were called and the manager expressed his concern about another resident of the same apartment block who attended the Institute, 33 year-old Linda Jarman who had also not been attending her classes. She was found nude and dead in her apartment with her television and car missing.

Police enquiries at the Institute found that an Art Teacher, Daniel Spence, had expressed his attraction towards Sherri Weathers to other staff and his advances had been rebuffed by Sherri herself. Spence had also been missing from classes since February 20th. The Institute were not unduly concerned about Spence as he was working for 'free' hoping to impress and gain a permanent paid position.

Fingerprints from the Talladega murders were identified as those of Daniel Siebert and Siebert's mug shot identified as that of the man known as Daniel Spence by the staff at the Institute. Siebert was known to police and had a conviction for manslaughter in Las Vegas in 1979, he was paroled in 1985 and was currently being sought for first degree assault in San Fransisco. He was also currently being sought under suspicion after a Talladega waitress, Linda Odum, 32, had gone missing on February 24th. Her car had been found dumped near Elizabeth Town, Kentucky on March 3rd, 1986 with his fingerprints inside the vehicle. Her naked and decomposed remains would later be found outside Talladega on March 30th. Officers were also keen to interview Siebert about the killing by strangulation of a prostitute in Calhoun County who was found shortly after he left his position at the Institute.

A nationwide hunt was on for Siebert and various sightings were reported in Ohio, Nevada, New Jersey, California and even as far away as Montreal, Canada.

The first definite lead came from an acquaintance of Siebert's who told police of a phone call from him on September 3rd. The call was traced to a pay-phone in Nashville, Tennessee and employees at a nearby restaurant identified him as a handyman working for the restaurant for cash. He was arrested the next day when he arrived for work.

Arrested and under caution Siebert confessed to five murders in Alabama and several others throughout America estimating that he could have killed twelve or more women in total. His reason for killing them was that he had been charged with assault by a San

Francisco prostitute after she survived an attempt to strangle her and he didn't want to go to prison again so the best way was to be careful and kill them all.

Siebert was also charged with the murders of 28 year old Gidget Castro and Nesia McElrath, 23, previously attributed to the South Side Slayers, a number of killers operating in the Los Angeles area in the 1980s. A further charge of murder for the killing of Beatrice McDougal in Atlantic city, New Jersey in 1986 was brought and several other unsolved murders in Arizona, California, Nevada and Florida were taken from the cold case files and re-opened.

A specimen charge of murder was made and on March 21st 1987, Siebert was convicted of Linda Jarman's murder in Talladega and given the death sentence in Alabama. After exhausting all of his appeals the sentence was never carried out as Siebert died in Holman prison from pancreatic cancer on April 22nd, 2008 age 53 after 21 years on Death Row.

# CORNELIUS SINGLETON

Born April 14th, 1956 – executed by electrocution in Alabama November 20, 1992.

One of the most worrying cases of a possible miscarriage of justice involving racial discrimination.

On November 12th 1977 Sister Ann Hogan, a Roman Catholic Nun, took her usual walk in a Mobile, Alabama, Cemetery and, as she always did, she knelt in prayer for the departed. At some stage during her walk or at prayer she was attacked and murdered by strangulation with her body being dragged into a wooded area and buried under stones and logs.

There was no evidence to connect Cornelius Singleton, 21, a black American, to the murder and no evidence that he knew the victim, had any motive to kill her or that he was even in the cemetery that day. But the local police arrested and charged him. Singleton, had an IQ of 45 ( a seven year old's IQ), could not read or write and had one previous conviction for arson in 1972 for which he had served 3 years..

So, these were the issues that were salient to the case:

1) There was nothing placing Singleton near the crime or linking him to the crime or the victim.
2) He had no motive.
3) Several eyewitnesses in or near the cemetery identified a white male with blonde hair acting suspiciously on the day. He was never found.
4) No other suspects were interviewed.

5) Singleton unknowingly waived his right to counsel.

6) Singleton signed a dictated confession. He thought he was confessing to stealing a bed sheet from his lodgings.

7) In order to level a charge of capital crime the prosecution needed evidence of an additional crime. A watch allegedly stolen from the Nun had failed to be found but on a very quick *second* search the police found it on a mantel at Singleton's grandfather's house. His grandfather stated it was not there the day before the second search.

8) No forensic evidence linked the crime to Singleton. Despite blood on the Nun's blouse it was not tested for comparison to Singleton's blood group.

9) His first trial attorney failed to use his retardation as a mitigating factor to ask for life in prison rather than a death sentence.

The all white jury found Singleton guilty of capital murder. Appeals were granted on the basis of the points above and in the end Singleton was retried in 1981 with a different all white jury and found guilty again. He had never met the attorney who handled his appeals and whilst on Death Row had no meeting with any attorney to discuss further appeals. Basically the State of Alabama failed to protect Singleton's right to a fair and impartial trial free from racial discrimination. The Alabama State and Federal Appeals courts, including the U.S. Supreme Court, failed to rectify this failure.

Singleton was executed by electrocution at Holman prison, Alabama, on November 20th, 1992 aged 36, 15 years after the Nun's murder.

# ROBERT LEE TARVER Jr.

Born 1947 – executed by electrocution in Alabama on April 14th 2000.

On the evening of September 15th, 1984, Hugh Kite was closing up his store, Kite's Grocery and Bait Store in Cottonton together with a ten year old helper, Jerry Ford, Cottonton walked around to the back of the store to load a bag of ice into his truck when Ford heard three shots being fired. The helper waited until a customer, Bernie Davis, came to the store and told him what he had heard. Davis then took a flashlight round to the back of the store and found Kite on the ground. He called the police. The officer arrived from Russell County Sheriff's Office and found no pulse on the victim. He secured the scene and called the coroner's office, an ambulance and some back up. The community was shocked at the killing as Kite's store was a communal gathering place and local post office. Everybody knew him and his generosity.

It had been raining that day and distinctive shoe prints were noticed in the soft ground leading from the body across railroad tracks to a patch of waste land close to the store and also owned by Kite. New tire tracks were also found in the mud on the land which the shoe prints led to and from. The car had four different tires and was soon identified as belonging to Robert

Tarver. The car was parked outside his home in Pittsview when the police went to interview him.

Tarver was arrested together with accomplice Andrew Richardson who testified later at his trial that he had been drinking all evening with Tarver in the car which Tarver had parked on the waste ground. Richardson stated that Tarver had no money to buy more drink and had taken out a gun and walked towards the store. When he returned he gave Richardson $80 and said he *'had killed Kite'*. A beer can found near where the car had been parked yielded Tarver's fingerprints. The print from shoes he was wearing at the time of his arrest matched those found behind the store and on the waste ground. The police also recovered a pistol that had been lent to Tarver some time before that a ballistics report identified as the pistol used in Kite's killing.

Tarver decided to defend himself in court and was already on parole for a previous robbery conviction. The jury found him guilty of the murder of Hugh Kite and recommended a life sentence without parole. The judge overrode that and gave Tarver a death sentence which set off 15 years of appeals until Tarver went to the electric chair at Holman prison on April 14th 2000 age 52. Hugh Kite's son and daughter watched the execution out of sight of reporters that attended it. Tarver made eye contact twice with them without any attempt to communicate. They declined to comment afterwards.

Andrew Richardson received a 25 year sentence for First Degree Robbery and was eligible for parole in April 2001.

# WALLACE NORRELL THOMAS.

Born 1955 – executed by electrocution in Alabama July 13th, 1990.

On December 20th 1976 Quenette Shehane, 21, a white graduate at Auburn University went out to buy salad dressing from the local U-Tote-Em grocery store. It was dark and as she left the store she was abducted by three black men, Wallace Thomas, Edward Lee and Jerry Jones. Her screams were heard by people in the store who mistook them for children playing. Quenette was shoved into her own car by the three who drove off and kept her captive for four hours during which time they raped her. When the three had finished Thomas told them that she had to be killed because all three had used each other's names and she would be able to identify them. They turfed her naked out of the car into the freezing night and Thomas shot her as she tried to run away with all three laughing and shouting. Her body was found frozen solid the next day. Her dumped car was quickly found and yielded forensic proof of the identities of the three men by way of prints and dry semen residue on the seats.

In custody Lee and Jones accused Thomas of instigating the whole thing and of the fatal shooting of Quenette. At trial both Lee and Jones were given life sentences for first degree rape and Thomas sentenced to death for capital murder with other charges of abduction and rape held on file. His execution was repeatedly delayed by a series of appeals until he was finally executed by electrocution at Holman prison on July 13$^{th}$ 1990, age 35, fourteen years after the killing.

Quenette Shehane's mother, Miriam became Alabama's leading advocate for victims' rights founding a group of like minded people called Victims of Crime and Leniency, promoting the rights of families of murder victims. In a newspaper interview she said *'I have always believed in the death penalty. I had always wondered in the back of my mind that if I was on a jury and had the responsibility of giving out the death penalty would I be able to do so. Now I know that I would be able to do so, and I know why it is so important.'*

# MICHAEL EUGENE THOMPSON

Born June 30th, 1959 – executed by lethal injection in Alabama on March 13th, 2003.

On December 10th, 1984 Maisie Gray, 57, was working at the Majik-Mart store in Attalla, it was her third week working there after months of looking for employment. That evening Michael Thompson, 25, came into the store and pointed a .22 calibre pistol at Maisie ordering her to open the cash register and pass him the notes. Fearing she had recognised him and would identify him to law enforcement Thompson then ordered Maisie into the boot of his car and drove out of the area. He eventually stopped near a dry well in Blount County and forced Maisie into it before shooting down into it until he ran out of ammunition. He then drove back to Shirley Franklin, his girlfriend's house and taking more ammunition returned with her to the well and whilst Franklin held a torch he fired more bullets into Maisie's still body at the bottom of the well. The next day he cleaned the pistol and threw it down another well.

On January 5th the next year, 1985, Franklin's estranged husband rang law enforcement saying he knew where Maisie's body was and who had killed her. When officers went to his house Shirley Franklin was there and told them Thompson was the killer and where to find the body. She made and signed a written statement which allowed the officers to arrest Thompson after they had recovered the body. At first he denied the charge but after a jail visit from Shirley

Franklin a day later he gave a taped confession stating the reason for the initial robbery was to get money to buy Christmas presents but Maisie had told him she knew who he was and where he lived so he had to kill her. The police and Maisie Gray's family dispute this.

It later became known that Shirley Franklin told Thompson in her jail visit that if he confessed the charge of murder against her which would send her to the electric chair would be dropped. Whether there was ever a charge of murder against her is disputed as at most she was an accessory after the fact but it may have been threatened by the police to get her to elicit Thompson to confess. We will never know. What we do know is that before this Shirley Franklin had a criminal history of armed robbery and had escaped three times from an Indiana prison whilst serving an eight year sentence.

Thompson was convicted of capital murder on May 10$^{th}$, 1985 with the jury recommending the death penalty which the judge duly agreed with and handed down. The appeals system ended when the U.S Supreme court declined to review the conviction in 1987. It took 19 years from the time of the murder to Thompson's execution in March 2003 by lethal injection at Holman prison, Alabama aged 43.

During his imprisonment Thompson wrote to the Canadian Coalition to Abolish the Death Penalty:

*Dear Friends:*
*My name is Michael Thompson. I'm a forty year old white male, and a prisoner on Alabama's death row.*

*I was arrested, convicted, and sentenced to death for a crime I did not commit. I was just twenty-five years of age when I was arrested on January 5, 1985, over fifteen years ago.*

*While the details of the events are very complicated and have never been allowed to be told, essentially when I was arrested for the crime the police "tricked" me by telling me that my live-in girl was also under arrest, charged with the crime, and would be executed unless I gave a "confession" that I committed the crime. Out of determination to obtain a confession the police engaged in these "threats" against her life and "promises" to release her in exchange for the confession. She was brought in to see me, wearing handcuffs, weeping, professing her love for me, and begging me to "save her life", even though she was never under arrest, and was acting as an agent for the police to help force a false confession from me.*

*Prior to my arrest I had a record that consisted of some fifteen traffic violations that occurred in three separate traffic stops. No felony convictions. My live-in girlfriend was eleven years my senior, twice convicted of armed robbery, spent eight years in an Indiana State Prison, escaping prison three times, and was wanted for armed robbery as she conspired with the police to frame me for the crime in question. The crime was a month old and the police had no leads until she came forward and led them to the victim's body, telling them that I committed the crime.*

*The police were desperate to solve the crime, and acting on her word they rushed to arrest me, and to force a confession from me, despite my invoking my*

*Constitutional Rights to remain silent, to receive counsel, and a telephone call. My invocation of mv rights was recorded onto the Miranda waiver sheet, witnessed by a second investigator and filed.*

*Then the police very aggressively proceeded to interrogate me in repeated waves for over twenty-four hours in direct violation of my Constitutional Rights. When I continued to invoke my right, refusing to talk to the police, requesting an attorney and a telephone call, the police became very frustrated and designed the plan to use Promises, Threats, and Trickery that involved my live-in girlfriend. Having been held for over twenty-four hours "incommunicado" ,put through waves of brutal interrogations, I finally agreed to say whatever they desired in exchange for her release, so that she could retain counsel for me as she promised.*

*The courts consider a "confession" the most damning evidence possible against a defendant. so the investigators will stoop to any level necessary to obtain a confession. They also cover up evidence that will jeopardize the validity of the confession, such as they did in my case when they failed to produce the waiver of rights sheet that recorded my refusal to waive my rights. in defiance of the court's order that all evidence both for and against be produced. However, the court itself helped in the prosecution's illegal actions by denying me a pre-trial suppression hearing in which to challenge the voluntariness of the confession. The court, midway through the trial, simply allowed the confession into evidence under a "collateral benefit" doctrine that the Supreme Court had rejected some years prior.*

*Court appointed defense attorneys never attempted to even mount a defense since the prosecution would present the confession. They simply pled me guilty to capital murder in their opening statement, begging the jury to spare my life.*

*The State's key witness, my ex-girlfriend, took the stand to testify against me. During recess the victim of her armed robbery made a positive identification that she was indeed the woman who had put a gun to his head and threatened to "blow his brains out ". The entire court knew this. However, she was not arrested for the crime, because it would have destroyed her testimony as the State's key witness. Furthermore, she was paid some $11,000 in reward money for her services, and after the trial was able to erase her entire life long record. Professional investigation companies were unable to find that she ever existed.*

*It took me many years of worthless, wasted appeals in the State appeals courts before I was allowed to appeal to the Federal Courts. On November 13, 1997, I attended a Federal District Court hearing on the voluntariness of the confession...my first opportunity to really challenge the confession, and the Federal Judge was so moved by the evidence that he issued a verbal ruling that day, ruling the confession "Involuntary" i.e., a product of promises, threats, and trickery, and illegally obtained. I was wrongfully convicted. However even though the Federal Judge ruled the confession "involuntary", two years and three months later (as of March 1, 2000), I still sit on death row as if nothing happened. Having ruled that I was wrongfully convicted, you would think that the Judge would be eager to correct the injustice that has been done.*

*My Pro Bono attorneys have taken a "do nothing" position, and they will not respond to my letters of concern, leaving me with no legal assistance nor advice. I should be a free man today, but due to the Judge's negligence and passive attorneys I still sit on death row condemned to die. How does a United States Federal Court Judge rule verbally that a man was wrongfully, convicted by the use of an illegal, involuntary confession, yet still fail to correct the wrong that was done twenty-seven months later?*

*I've come to realize that I'm in dire need of competent, diligent, aggressive attorneys who will press for resolve. Having no means in which to hire competent attorneys who will pursue my best interests, I am left sitting on death row, wrongfully convicted, ruled so by a Federal Court Judge, yet still helplessly condemned to death! This wrongful conviction has stolen over fifteen years of my life, and I am no closer to my freedom than I was fifteen years ago, despite the Federal Court's ruling that I was in fact wrongfully convicted by use of an illegal, involuntary confession, a product of promises, threats, and trickery. Where's MY justice? I'm a United States citizen, and I'm entitled to the protections guaranteed under the Constitution.*

*The very same investigators who did this to me have caused that county to have to pay millions of dollars in law suits for the same illegal actions used against other innocent men in other cases. Their record speaks for itself Terrorism is their normal procedure for solving cases, and what they do is no different than putting a gun to the head of a loved one and demanding false confessions in exchange for their life,*

*It's become blatantly obvious to me that national exposure is required in order to force the wheels of justice along, and hopefully help me to obtain competent, aggressive legal assistance who will pursue my ultimate freedom from this wrongful conviction. I would deeply appreciate any and all support that is offered on my behalf. "Remember them that are in bonds. as though bound with them; and them which suffer adversity, as being yourselves also in the body." (Hebrews 13:3)*

*Thank you, Michael Thompson.*

# STEVEN ALLEN THOMPSON

Born 1964 – executed by electrocution in Alabama May 8$^{th}$ 1988.

This is one the most sadistic murder cases ever.

The following is the trial judge's verbatim statement of facts which I think tells this awful story better than I can:

*The victim, Robin Balarzs, was engaged to marry David Roberts, a long-time friend of the defendant. On May 11, 1984, David Roberts was absent from Huntsville due to military service. His friend Steven Thompson was aware of this absence.*
*On that day Thompson went to the home in Huntsville where Robin Balarz resided with her parents and her three year old son. The parents and the child were also out of town. Only Robin and her friend Cindy McElroy were at the residence. Thompson, Robin and Cindy engaged in normal conversation and Thompson stayed over and slept on a sofa while the girls retired to separate bedrooms.*
*Early on the morning of May 12th Thompson left the residence. Cindy McElroy left at a later time. Cindy noticed no unusual behaviour on the part of Thompson.*
*At that time, Thompson was absent without leave from the Navy and had need of money or goods which he could sell for cash. He planned to return to the Balarzs household to feloniously take money, gold or*

*silver.* In his planning Thompson bought tape, bandages and other items with which to bind Robin.

On his arrival back at the house in the night of May 12th, 1984, Thompson entered the household on invitation of his friend and followed a course of conduct which can be described as beyond human comprehension in its vileness.

Thompson bound and gagged Robin with a sock, bandage, rope and tape he had brought into her home with premeditated design. He cut her clothes from her person and beat her with his fists. He took a meagre $1.00 bill from her purse (although at some point he also took her engagement ring). He stuffed a sock in her mouth. He cut her with a knife. He then positioned his rental vehicle near the garage to facilitate her removal from the residence.

He made some effort to conceal the blood and physical tracings of his acts of brutality, he placed Robin, still alive, in the vehicle, left the home and drove to secluded Green Mountain, a rugged area in Huntsville, Madison County. There, he proceeded to brutalize Robin Balarzs in a manner almost unspeakable in its nature, character and extent.

Thompson had sexual intercourse upon her, shoved a large knife into what he thought to be her vagina, bound her breasts with a rope, tied her to the vehicle and dragged her through mud, over rocks and on pavement for a distance in excess of 3000 feet. At some point he pulled and shaved her hair with a razor especially purchased. He stabbed her about her breasts and cut her with the knife.

Robin Balarzs died during her ordeal. Some of the atrocities were against her corpse.

The defendant realized that left in the Balarzs's home were items which would reveal his crimes, if not his identity. He returned to the residence for the purpose of securing these items, leaving Robin Balarzs on Green Mountain.

While Thompson was attempting to re-enter the Balarzs home David Roberts returned. Seeing David drive up to the residence, Thompson evaded detection and drove away to spend the rest of the night in his vehicle.

David Roberts entered the home and noticed signs of Thompson's depravity. He contacted neighbors and friends of Robin, called hospitals and tried to locate her. Finally, David Roberts called Huntsville Police Department and investigation into the case began. David recalled seeing Thompson's vehicle parked near the residence and an alert was dispatched on Thompson by radio. At that time it was in connection with a missing person report.

In the early morning of May 13, 1984, two uniformed officers saw Thompson in his vehicle and stopped him. The vehicle was dirty and damaged and Thompson had what appeared to be blood and mud about his person. Thompson was properly advised of his constitutional rights, taken into custody, removed to police headquarters and questioned.

After first denying knowledge of the fate of Robin Balarzs, Thompson made statements admitting his activities and led an officer to the scene atop Green Mountain. Robin's battered body was found. Her *parents and David Roberts were advised that she was dead.*

*After his arrest, Thompson made two statements to police. On the day of his arrest, Thompson described the events that occurred at Balarzs' house. He also described dragging Balarzs to his car, putting her in the backseat, placing a sleeping bag over her, and driving her to Green Mountain. Thompson told the police that Balarzs "moaned and groaned" during the drive to Green Mountain.*

*The next morning, Thompson gave police another statement. Thompson described in more detail the events at Balarzs's home. Thompson told police that Balarzs was bleeding and vomit was coming out of her mouth when he took her out of the car on Green Mountain. Thompson told police he had sexual intercourse with Balarzs and then described thrusting a butcher's knife into her vaginal area, tying her to his car, and dragging her body.*

On August 9$^{th}$, 1985 a jury convicted Thompson of robbery-murder, kidnapping-murder and rape-murder. By an 8 to 4 vote they recommended a life sentence without parole. The court overrode the jury's recommendation and sentenced Thompson to death by electrocution.

Thompson was sent to the electric chair at Holman prison on May 8$^{th}$. 1998 after waiving his right to any last minute appeal saying he wanted to spare any further pain to his family and his victim's family. Robin Balarzs's son was taken into care by her mother.

# BILLY WAYNE WALDROP

Born 1952 – executed by electrocution in Alabama on January 10th, 1997.

During the night of June 2$^{nd}$, 1982 Thurman Donahoo, 72, was robbed of just $130 and a valuable 5 carat diamond ring, he was beaten and shot before being left for dead in his 100 year old house in Alpine, Talladega County, Alabama which was then set on fire and burnt to the ground. Donahoo's charred body was almost unrecognizable when found in the ashes. Suspicion for the perpetrator of the crime fell immediately on Billy Waldrop. Donahoo's murder was less than two years after Waldrop finished serving seven years for the 1973 killing and torturing of two men in Calhoun County where his initials were found carved on one victim's body.

Three weeks after the arson in July, 1982, Waldrop was arrested in California on a drunk driving charge and was returned to Alabama where a warrant had been issued for his arrest charging him with receipt of stolen property. That property being the diamond ring stolen from Donahoo, which Waldrop had sold for $10,000 and some intense detective work by the Alabama police had recovered it in a Tennessee jewellers together with a receipt for the money paid for it signed by Waldrop as the 'owner' of the ring. He was taken to Talladega County where he gave a statement implicating himself and two others in the Donahoo robbery and murder.

The two others were Eugene Singleton and Henry Mays. Waldrop claimed it was Singleton who shot Donahoo. This was contested by both Singleton and Mays who both accused Waldrop of having the gun and killing Donahoo. After their 1983 trials Singleton served 10 years for burglary at Donahoo's home and was paroled in 1994. Mays died whilst awaiting trial on the same charge. Waldrop was charged with capital murder and was found guilty on February 18$^{th}$, 1983 with a jury recommendation of the death penalty to the judge. On the sentencing hearing on March 22$^{nd}$ the court administered the death penalty on Waldrop. The Alabama Court of Criminals Appeals upheld the sentence as did the U.S. Supreme Court. Waldrop went to the electric chair in Holman prison, Alabama, on January 10$^{th}$, 1997, fifteen years after the murder of Thurman Donahoo and then aged 44. Apparently he sang 'Amazing Grace' as he waited for the jolt.

# VARNELL WEEKS

Born May 10th, 1952 – executed by electrocution in Alabama May 12th, 1995.

This case resurrected the arguments in Alabama in the 1990's against giving the death penalty to mentally ill or mentally retarded people after it had been reinstated in the county in 1983.

In 1981 Varnell Weeks robbed and murdered college student Mark Batts, 24, who was studying veterinary science at Tuskegee Institute. Weeks fled the scene and was arrested after a gun battle with the police in which one officer, David Dearden, was badly wounded suffering life changing injuries.

Weeks had spent time in mental institutions in the 1970s and psychiatrists from both the state prosecution and the defence had diagnosed him as suffering from paranoid schizophrenia with symptoms including delusions and hallucinations. None of this was disclosed at his trial for the Mark Batts murder. Once he had been convicted he waived his right to appeal and jury sentencing and asked for the electric chair.

Prison records show he would stand naked in his cell and smear himself with excrement whilst making indecipherable sounds. At a hearing to determine his competency for execution he appeared with a domino on a string tied round his head and rambled on about albinos, Egyptians, the Bible and other unrelated subjects. He told people in prison that he was God and his execution would destroy mankind and he himself would become a giant turtle and rule the universe.

Obviously, none of this was available at the time of his trial. The legal appeals all rejected his attorney's request for a stay of execution on the grounds that although he was mentally ill he was mentally competent and that he understood the crime he was convicted of and why he was sentenced to die.

Varnell Weeks was electrocuted at Holman prison on May 12$^{th}$, 1995, 14 years after he murdered Mark Batts and at age 43.

David Dearden, the police officer injured in the shoot out with Weeks had just one comment for the press on the execution, *'Fry him.'*

# THOMAS WARREN WHISENHANT

Born January 29$^{th}$, 1947 – executed by lethal injection in Alabama May 27$^{th}$, 2010.

On October 16$^{th}$, 1976 Whisenhant, age 29, entered a Compact Store in Theodore, robbed the cash register and kidnapped the store clerk on duty, 23 year old Cheryl Payton, a mother of two. He took her in his pickup truck to a wooded area in Mobile County where he raped her in the truck before killing her by shooting her in the head with a .32 pistol in a field beside the truck and then dragged her body into the woods. Whisenhant returned to the body two days later and cut off a large section of her breast and cut open her stomach. He was seen there by people who were out searching for Paynton after she had been listed as missing the day before who called the police. Whisenhant ran off into the woods and hid only emerging after his wife was brought to the scene and using a loudspeaker implored him to give himself up which he did shouting to her *'I've done everything they said I did.'*

Taken into custody and charged with Payton's murder Whisenhant surprised the officers by claiming two previous murders in Mobile County, Alabama, during the previous 18 months, Venora Hyatt and Patricia Hitt.

Thomas Warren Whisenhant was born on January 29, 1947, in Prichard, Alabama, the last of four children born to Willie and Emma Whisenhant. He came from a low-income family which was ruled by his mother, a domineering woman who would constantly argue with and frequently attack her physically weak and alcoholic husband and who also encouraged her children to do the same. Such altercations often occurred when Whisenhant's father would get drunk on moonshine and try to seduce his wife, who would always reject him. She reserved her anger and abuse only for her husband and instead spoiled Whisenhant, of whom she was overprotective. Whisenhant was made to share a bed with his mother until the age of 7 and continued to share the same bedroom with her until the age of 16, by which time he had, according to his sister, become moody and violent. Also in his teenage years, Whisenhant was constantly accompanied by his mother for some reason, who never let him out of her sight. According to a psychologist this caused Whisenhant to resent her.

On May 6, 1963, 13years before the Payton murder, 72-year-old widow Lexie Haynes was fatally shot in Prichard. Police arrived at the scene and found the murder weapon in an empty lot next to Whisenhant's family home. Whisenhant, who was 16 at the time, was immediately suspected, as he had recently been charged with robbing a blind woman. According to a retired Prichard police captain, the robbery charge against Whisenhant was later thrown out of court due to a technicality. Police questioned Whisenhant about the murder; however, his family provided him with an alibi and claimed he had been at home when the shooting occurred. Before the shooting occurred, Whisenhant and his friends had been playing with a stolen handgun. A witness later said Whisenhant had taken a bullet from the revolver, held it up, and stated it would soon kill somebody. Police later revealed that Haynes had spoken with Whisenhant about this behavior, which was why they suspected he killed her. However, for unknown reasons, Whisenhant was never brought to trial for the murder of Haynes.

Whisenhant joined the United States Air Force and was based at Colorado. On October 25th, 1965 he attacked 22 year-old Rose Covington, a U.S. Air Force WAF beating her unconscious. They had never previously met. Whisenhant denied the attack but his shoe prints were found at the scene and he was convicted of assault with intent to commit murder on March 14th, 1966 and received 20 years in prison with hard labour. The sentence was reduced on appeal in 1970 to ten years and he was granted parole on November 28th, 1973.

On November 21st, 1975 he attacked Patricia Hitt, a mother of two who was working at a convenience store in Mobile County, Alabama, beating her before shooting her in the head killing her. On April 16th, 1976, he murdered again at a convenience store in Mobile, kidnapping and shooting 44 year old Venora Hyatt before dumping her body in an abandoned shed in Mobile. He returned to the shed the following day and mutilated the body taking Hyatt's wristwatch which he gave to his wife as a present.

Whisenhant was tried for the murder of Payton on August 1st 1977. He pleaded not guilty by reason of insanity. The jury found him guilty of capital murder and on September 7th he was sentenced to death. The Alabama Court of Criminal Appeals reversed this decision and he was retried in 1981 and convicted again.

Once more the decision was overturned due to a remark made by the prosecution and once more he was retried and convicted in 1987.

Whisenhant's appeals went on until May 27$^{th}$, 2010 when he was executed by lethal injection at Holman prison, Alabama when the U.S. Supreme Court refused a stay of execution and the Alabama Governor refused a request for clemency. At the time of his execution Whisenhant was 63 and Alabama's longest serving Death Row prisoner having spent thirty-two years, eight months and twenty days on Death Row.

# LEROY B. WHITE

Born November 28th 1958 – executed by lethal injection in Alabama on January 12th, 2011.

Leroy White and his wife Ruby, a first grade Elementary School teacher, had a marriage that had broken down. Leroy White couldn't accept this and the fact that he had been told by Ruby's divorce lawyer to vacate their West Huntsville home at 22717 Evan's Drive, which was owned by Ruby. So angry was he that when the divorce was filed in August 1988 he took a .38 calibre pistol and shot her in the leg. Ruby did not press charges.

In the afternoon of October 17th, having vacated the property in Evan's Drive, West Huntsville, White returned later that day carrying a pistol and a shotgun which he had bought at the Blue Springs Pawn Shop and shotgun ammunition that he had bought at Larry's Pawn Shop. His intention to shoot Ruby was obvious. He shot open the front door with the shotgun and was approached by Ruby's sister, Stella Lanier, who was in the house with Ruby. He shot Stella in the chest and shoulder with the pistol before going back to his car and reloading the shotgun. He then went back into the house looking for Ruby who managed to run out of the front door before White shot her in the back and she fell to the ground. He went again to the car and reloaded before telling Ruby, *'Bitch, you ain't dead yet.'* and then shooting her again, four times, and killing her.

The jury at his trial found him guilty of capital murder and voted 9-3 to recommend to the judge that he served life in prison without parole. The judge overruled the jury and sentenced White to death describing White's actions as *'heinous and atrocious compared to other capital offences.'*

Leroy White was executed by lethal injection on January 13th, 2011 at Holman prison, Alabama, after exhausting the appeals available and his attorney's last appeal to the U.S. Supreme Court being dismissed. He was 53 and had been on Death Row for 23 years.

# JIMMY EARL WHITT

Born 1971 – committed suicide by shooting himself after being surrounded by law enforcement officers on June 28$^{th}$, 1994.

Jimmy Whitt, 23, was from Mobile, Alabama and had been living in Miami before going on a murder spree in June 1994 taking the lives of three officers and a store clerk.

The first killings were on June 14$^{th}$ in the town of Greenville. Whitt robbed a store and shot and killed the clerk Pamella Scruggs and police officer Gary Heath who attended the alarm call. Whitt made off taking Officer Heath's gun with him. The next day he was seen in South Mississippi driving a stolen rental car that had been used in a Hotel robbery in Miami on June 8th. He was pulled over by 23 year old Len Rowell, a deputy with the Pearl River County Sheriff's Department, who he shot and killed. Whitt was identified as the suspect and later on that day he was spotted 70 miles away in Mobile where he stole another car and drove off on interstate 1-10. Twenty five miles further on he stopped at the Loxley exit and was approached by Coy Smith, 61, an Alabama PSC Officer. He shot Smith several times as he sat in his patrol car calling in Whitt's car tag, killing him. Whitt then drove south towards Foley where he parked in a McDonald's drive through where he approached Donna Akers in her car with her two children and tried to steal the vehicle. She resisted and he shot her and drove off in the same car as he came into the McDonald's in. He was spotted as he headed back towards Loxley and police vehicles surrounded his moving car on the road. An agent in a marked car pulled alongside Whitt and motioned him with a gun to pull over. Whitt smiled and put a gun to his temple and committed suicide.

# JASON ORIC WILLIAMS

Born April 16th, 1968 – executed by lethal injection in Alabama on May 19th, 2011.

Jason Oric Williams was adopted by his aunt and uncle at infancy. His aunt and uncle did not disclose to Williams that they were not his biological parents. Williams grew up in poverty, performed poorly academically, and felt he was snubbed by his family and peers. When he turned seventeen years old, he attempted to obtain identification documents so that he could work. It was during this process that Williams learned that he was adopted. This news devastated Williams, and he began experimenting with alcohol and drugs such as LSD, crack, marijuana, ecstacy, and prescription medications.

In 1990, Williams married Sandra Ellzey. Williams and Ellzey remained married for about ten months, divorcing in 1991due to Williams violent behaviour. He had slapped Ellzey in the face many times, pulled her hair, and broken her glasses. Williams, however, continued to live with Ellzey after they were divorced. In January 1992, Ellzey discovered needles for drug use in her home, and learned that Williams had been injecting tranquilizers. Ellzey then asked Williams to leave.

On February 15th, 1992 Williams, age 23, spent the evening in local bars drinking heavily and taking drugs before returning to the trailer home of Gerald Paravicini, his wife and stepson. Paravicini had taken Williams in a fortnight earlier when Ellzey had kicked him out of their marital home. When Paravicini's son opened the door to him Williams shot him in the face with an automatic .22 rifle before walking inside and shooting Gerald Paravicini in the chest and neck killing him. He then smashed Clair Paravicini in the face with the butt of the rifle breaking her jaw before stealing her purse, credit cards and $530 in cash. Clair and her son both survived the attack.

Williams then went to the home of neighbours Fred and Linda Barber nearby. He shot Linda in the face when she opened the door killing her instantly before shooting dead her husband and her son, Bryan 22, who was asleep in his bedroom. Another son, Brad, 16, grappled with Williams and escaped with a bullet wound to his hand.

Williams then stole the family van, cash and credit cards and made off. After a police chase he was stopped in Mississippi, he was unarmed having thrown the rifle from a bridge and denied knowing anything about the shootings. The gun was never recovered.

On April $12^{th}$, 1992, Williams was indicted on two counts of capital murder and two of attempted murder. On November $11^{th}$, 1992 the jury returned guilty verdicts and recommended by 10-2 that a death penalty be imposed. On December $1^{st}$ the State trial court sentenced Williams to a punishment of death.

Williams was executed at Holman prison, Alabama by lethal injection on May $19^{th}$ 2011. Nineteen years after the killings and after exhausting the appeals system when the U.S. Supreme Court refused a stay of execution and dismissed his final appeal.

Williams was the first person in Alabama to be executed using the drug pentobarbital instead of sodium thiopental in its lethal injection cocktail after the manufacturer of sodium thiopental ceased production of the drug. As a result several states switched to pentobarbital, a sedative used to euthanize animals.

# LUTHER JEROME WILLIAMS

Born November 15$^{th}$, 1959 – executed by lethal injection in Alabama on August 23$^{rd}$, 2007.

On January 22$^{nd}$, 1988, a dark blue Oldsmobile Regency was stolen from a hotel parking area in Birmingham, Alabama. In the boot was a .22 calibre pistol. The next time the vehicle was seen was when it was parked at the Smithfield housing project in Birmingham later that evening with Jerome Williams, 28, sitting in it.

On the morning of January 23$^{rd}$, 1988, John Kirk, 63, was on his way home from work in his red 1984 Chevrolet pickup with a camper on the back on the Interstate 59 South when the motor developed engine trouble and he pulled it off the road near the West Blocton exit in Tuscaloosa County. Coming the other way was Williams in the stolen Oldsmobile with two friends, Albert Charmichael and Trosky Gregory. They stopped and at some time after that Williams led John Kirk into a nearby wooded area and shot him in the head killing him. They then stole money he had on him, his watch and the vehicle.

Again Williams was seen and identified as being in the camper vehicle on the Smithfield housing project later that day. He boasted to a neighbour that he had killed a white man and stolen his truck. He showed the gun to Priscilla Jones, a relative. Jones told another member of the family who called the police who interviewed Jones and after that interview they identified Williams as the driver and that he was staying at an apartment in the housing project and was already a wanted person after absconding from a supervised intensive restitution programme. On January 25$^{th}$, 1988 they arrested him at his girlfriend's mother's apartment and made a search which recovered the gun used to kill John Kirk.

Williams was indicted on April 29$^{th}$ for the murder of John Kirk. He had 15 previous convictions for burglary, armed robbery and assault already on file. The trial began on November 27$^{th}$, 1989 and the jury returned a guilty verdict on November 30$^{th}$ recommending the death penalty which the judge agreed with. William's two accomplices pleaded guilty to lesser charges of being present at a robbery resulting in killing and were both given life in prison with parole opportunities. Both had testified against Williams identifying him as the one who killed John Kirk.

Williams was executed at Holman prison on August 23$^{rd}$, 2007 age 48 after spending 19 years on Death Row after the U.S. Supreme Court dismissed an appeal against the guilty verdict. He always insisted that Gregory and Charmichael had been promised life sentences with parole instead of execution only if they testified against him and that he was not the killer.

# HOLLY WOOD

Born July 4th, 1960 – executed by lethal injection in Alabama on September 10th, 2010.

This is a straightforward murder case. Wood, 33, was on parole for shooting a former girlfriend, Barbara Siler, and had 18 previous arrests on his criminal record when he killed Ruby Gosha, another girlfriend and mother of his child.

On the night of September 1st, 1993 at around 5pm Wood was told by Ruby's mother that he was not welcome at her house where Ruby was staying and to leave and not visit again. He had previously assaulted Ruby who had split with him.

Wood left and at around 9pm returned with a 12-gauge shotgun and shot Ruby before running off. Ruby died in the ambulance on the way to hospital. Wood boasted to his cousin, Calvin Salter later that night that *'I shot the bitch and blew her brains out'*

Wood was arrested the same night and held in custody. At his trial for murder on October 20th, 1994 Wood was found guilty with the jury recommending the death sentence by a 10-2 vote. The judge upheld this recommendation.

Wood exhausted all his appeals and was executed by lethal injection on September 10th, 2010 at Holman prison, Alabama, 17 years after the murder.

# FREDDIE LEE WRIGHT

Born April 29$^{th}$, 1951 – executed by electrocution in Alabama on March 3$^{rd}$, 2000.

According to the prosecution attorneys Freddie Wright, Roger McQueen, Percy Craig and Reginald Tinsly were on their way to rob another convenience store when they stopped at the Western Auto Store in Mount Vernon, Alabama on December 1$^{st}$, 1977. They had stopped to buy some tape to use in their planned robbery elsewhere but once they were there decided to rob the Western Auto Store instead.

Inside were Warren and Lois Green, the owners, who were about to go off to celebrate Warren's 40$^{th}$ birthday. They were forced into the back room at gunpoint and bound together back to back before both being shot in the head at point blank range. McQueen, Tinsley and Craig all testified that Wright fired those fatal shots.

BUT, is this correct? A witness who was leaving the store identified another man, Theodore Robinson as going into the store and a parked vehicle, later identified as Robinson's, outside the store with *four men* inside. Robinson was briefly arrested and then released in connection with this crime.

Freddie Wright's letter of innocence below is very compelling and one has to ask why Robinson was excluded from the trial? Was it just a matter of Alabama justices not wanting a contrived police conviction to be overturned? The other three were all given convictions for murder and served sentences and are now released.

McQueen later recanted his testimony against Wright admitting it was in exchange for a prison sentence **with** parole.

Wright's first trial ended in a hung jury. He was sentenced to death at his second trial. The first trial was a mixed black and white jury, the second all white.

*SUMMARY OF FACTS RELATING TO MY INNOCENCE*
*TO WHOM IT MAY CONCERN WITH PROFOUND EXPRESSION OF MY REGARD.*
*I am a Alabama death row inmate that has nearly run the complete appellate gauntlet and am in dire need of any and all intervention. I have no doubt that because of recently publicized events in regards to death row inmates being found innocent of the crimes they have spent many years on death row for, the internet has been consumed by request such as my own.*

*Any attempt on my part to distinguish my case, from the many others innocent death row inmates now being housed throughout the United States would be futile. I can only stress, that because my case/appeals have reached the 11th Circuit Court of appeals and the overwhelming demands for your type of assistance, my options have run out.*

*Below I have briefly summarize the facts relating to my innocence each and everyone can be verified in their totality . . .*

*(1). I was convicted of murder and robbery at a local Western Auto Store, two individuals were killed. Stock was removed from the store by the assailants. Several of the stolen items were eventually recovered.*

*Another person Theodore Robinson was subsequently arrested and charged with these crimes.*

*(2). Ms. Charlene Tilton, at the time of the crime was the girlfriend of Mr. Robinson. Ms. Tilton gave a statement to Det. Stroh, which lead to Robinson's arrest, a weapon was discovered subsequent test of projectiles removed from the victims and test fired from the weapon by the Alabama Department of Forensic Science resulted in a "match".*

*(3). Ms. Mary Johnson, a patron of the local Western Auto Store was leaving the store as a man later identified as Mr. Robinson was entering. Ms. Johnson notices four (4), men in an automobile later identified as being owned by Robinson at the front entrance, a short period of time before the discovery of the victims. (a). Ms. Johnson, was summoned to testify at Mr. Robinson's preliminary hearing where she confirmed under oath the above. (b). Ms. Johnson has never testified to the above facts at any stage of my trials or hearing to this date.*

*(4). An individual whose name is unknown to myself, but was identified by the investigating officers as being in possession of items removed from the crime scene, identified Robinson as the person from whom he received the stolen goods. Inquiry into the investigative file will result in the accurate name of this individual.*

*(5). Roger McQueen and Percy Craig, initially implicated me as the shooter in this crime. Prior to trial both attempted to recant their statements. Their attempts were met with the threat of prosecution of this capital offense, which led them to again implicate me as an member of the ones who robbed the store.*

*(6). A third accomplice Mr. Reginald Tinsley, initially implicated me in this crime, but prior to trial on his own volition requested to give a statement to my trial counsel exonerating me of any involvement in this crime, before the prosecution had the chance to convince him otherwise.*

*(7). Additionally Mr. McQueen, stated under oath that we first met in the month of February 1978, some three (3) months after the crime occurred, making our participation in this crime together impossible.*

*(8). Ms. Doris Lambert, a former girlfriend of mine testified that during a June 1977 confession to her Catholic Priest stating that I confessed my involvement in this crime. The murder/robbery occurred six (6), months after her confession making her statement an obvious lie.*

*(9).* **The trial court judge issued an order for the exclusion of any and all testimony relating to Mr. Otis Theodore Robinson and his involvement in this crime. Which hindered my defense and the presentation of exculpatory evidence.**

*All of the above was requested vis motion of discovery by the defense counsel, but the prosecution and/or person having control and custody of these facts, either by act or lack of action failed to disclose the information which has lead to the technical exclusion otherwise known as procedural barring of evidence of my "actual innocence".*

*I am in desperately need of any and all help, if there is any additional information needed please do not hesitate to contact me. It's clear if I don't get help I am going' to lose my life, I await your response...*

*Sincerely, Freddie Lee Wright*

Freddie Wright went to the electric chair on March 3rd, 2000, twenty three years after the murders of Warren and Lois Green. We must not lose sight of the fact that two people were killed and their sixteen year old daughter ws left without parents.

# THE LADIES

## AMY BISHOP

Born April 24$^{th}$, 1965 – sentenced to life in prison without parole in Alabama on September 24$^{th}$, 2012.

Amy Bishop was a 44 year old mother of four and a well respected biology professor at the University of Alabama in Huntsville, Alabama. During a regular meeting of the Biology Department attended by 12 people on February 12$^{th}$, 2010 she suddenly, and without warning, stood up and began shooting those closest to her with a 9mm handgun working down the row. Three people were killed and another three hospitalised as a result of the spree. According to the Dean of the University's graduate program, Debra Moriaty, Bishop pointed the gun at her and it failed to fire. Together with others she then physically forced Bishop out of the room and locked the door. The police were called and arrested Bishop outside the building and recovered the gun from a staff washroom. She refused to accept what she had done as though her memory had been wiped telling the investigating officers, *'It didn't happen, no way, they are all alive.'*

Concern was expressed after the shooting that Bishop, who was working on herpes virus, may have planted a 'herpes' bomb somewhere in the university timed to go off and spread the virus. This scenario matched a plot used in one of her fiction novels. Bishop was an author of fiction with three unpublished novels and harboured thoughts of becoming a full time novelist as her tenure at the University was of limited time and she knew it was not being renewed. She was also the cousin of novelist John Irving and envied his life style. Others in the biology department had been concerned before about her behaviour which was very left field and even described as crazy and abrasive towards others which was the main reason her tenure was not being renewed.

Unknown to the University Bishop was already known to law enforcement. On December 6$^{th}$ 1986, when she was 21, she shot and killed her 18 year-old brother at their home in Braintree, Massachusetts firing three shots from a 12-gauge pump action shotgun. One shot went into a bedroom wall, one into her brother's chest and one into a ceiling she fled from the house. Both Amy and her mother described it all as accidental. The Braintree police investigated and came to the same conclusion and no charges were pressed. Detailed records of the incident had 'disappeared' when asked for in February, 2010 after the University spree. They miraculously re-appeared when searching questions were asked of senior officers and a cold case team were able to bring a charge of first degree murder against Bishop for her brother's killing nearly 24 years after the incident. The District Attorney commented that in the original investigation *'No excuses, jobs weren't done, responsibilities weren't met and justice wasn't served.'*

In 1993 Bishop and her husband were suspects in a letter-bomb case. Paul Rosenberg a physician at the Children's Hospital Boston received two pipe bombs in the post and luckily both failed to explode. Rosenberg had given a negative report on Amy Bishop's work at the hospital and had felt that *'she could not meet the standards required'*. The Bishop's denied the bombs had anything to do with them and refused to co-operate with investigators who didn't have enough evidence to warrant a search of their house. The case remains unsolved and on the file.

In 2002 Amy Bishop attacked and punched a lady who had taken the last seat at a restaurant yelling, *'I am Doctor Amy Bishop give me the seat.'* The prosecutor in the assault case suggested she took an anger management course. She didn't.

After the University killings Bishop was charged with one count of capital murder and three counts of attempted murder. If she was to be found guilty, according to Alabama State law, she was liable to either the death penalty or life in prison. Two days after being also indicted at the same time for the murder of her brother back in 1986 she attempted suicide in the Huntsville jail but survived and was deemed mentally and physically fit enough to remain in jail on suicide watch.

The families who lost relatives and those employees of the University who suffered injuries in Bishop's attack agreed with the prosecutor in her trial in 2012 that they could see no benefit in giving Bishop a sentence of death were she to be found guilty and the prosecutor offered life in prison if she were to plead guilty. On September 24th, 2012 she did so and received a life in prison sentence without parole. On the basis of this the charge of murdering her brother was dropped by the Massachusetts prosecutor as *'the penalty we would seek for a first degree murder conviction is already in place'*.

## LYNDA LYON BLOCK

See under male killer **GEORGE SIBLEY Jr.**

# EARLE C. DENNISON

Born 1900 – executed by electrocution at Kilby prison on September 4th, 1953.

(I haven't listed the killers back in the 50s/60s as information is sparse. But this one features a very unique scenario.)

Earle Dennison was the first ever white woman to be executed in Alabama. She was a nurse and a widow working at Wetumpka General Hospital in the surgery department. She had been there for 25 years.

Dennison had a married sister-in-law, Cora Weldon, who had two young children, a girl named Shirley and a boy named Orville. They lived in rural Elmore County.

On May 1st. 1952 Dennison paid them a visit. During that visit she gave Shirley a drink of orange. Shirley became ill and Dennison gave her a bottle of Coca-Cola. Shirley became worse and her mother rushed her to Wetumpka Hospital. The diagnosis was not good and it seemed Shirley was about to die.

Dennison heard this and left the hospital to drive to the home of a local insurance agent and paid an overdue premium on an insurance policy that was about to lapse that she had taken out of the little girl's life for $6,500. In today's money that is about $180,000.

Shirley didn't make it. An autopsy on the body revealed the presence of arsenic and a police investigation followed and found traces of the poison in the cup used for the orange drink and in the Coca-Cola bottle as well as in Shirley's vomit.

The existence of the insurance policy soon came to light as did another earlier episode bearing similar hallmarks. On the day Shirley was born Dennison was looking after her older sister Polly-Ann who became very ill after eating an ice cream given to her by Dennison. Polly-Ann was rushed into hospital but died. Nothing like foul play was suspected, after all Dennison was a nurse of great experience. No autopsy was carried out it was *'just one of those things'*.

After the death of their second child in similar circumstances to the death of their first Cora and her husband told the police of their suspicions. It was found that Dennison had profited from an insurance pay-out of $5,500 on the death of Polly-Ann. The child's body was exhumed and arsenic found in the tissues. Dennison's husband's body was also exhumed and tested, just in case, but no arsenic residue was found. Dennison was arrested and taken into custody where she admitted both murders. She attempted suicide in her cell with a razor blade but failed.

Her trial was set for August 14$^{th}$, 1952. The evidence was conclusive and the jury gave a guilty verdict and recommended a death sentence. Justice was swift in those days and Dennison went to the electric chair on September 4$^{th}$, 1953 age 55.

Cora Weldon later took the two insurance companies who issued the life policies on her children to court arguing that because Dennison had no 'insurable interest' in the children the companies should have been suspicious of her motives. She won and received $75,000 in settlement.

# TRACEY GRISSOM

Born 1982 – sentenced to 25 years in prison on September 2$^{nd}$, 2014.

Tracey Grissom, 30, had divorced from her husband Hunter Grissom, 27, with whom she had a 4 year old daughter. She alleged that after the split Hunter had been aggressive to her several times and on the last occasion had come to her house and brutally raped, sodomised and beaten her. She brought those charges against him and a trial was due.

On May 15$^{th}$. 2012, whilst driving to work at 8am Tracey saw Hunter working at a Binion Creek Boat Landing on Lake Tuscaloosa. She pulled up and told police she intended to take a photo of him working as he owed maintenance money for their child which he had said he couldn't afford as he was not working. According to witnesses when hunter saw his wife he gave her an obscene gesture. She left her car with a gun and emptied the whole magazine of bullets into him. Law officers responding to the 911 call found Hunter lying between the boat ramp and his vehicle dead in a pool of blood with the gun next to him where Tracey had dropped it. She was taken into custody, arrested and charged with murder. The case came to trial in August 2014 with the defence arguing that Tracey was suffering from post-traumatic stress disorder brought on by the earlier attack on her by Hunter. However the prosecution brought evidence that Tracey was in line to receive $103,000 from an insurance policy taken out during their marriage. This was countermanded by the defence stating that a part of their agreed divorce was that Hunter would pay Tracey $1,200 a month for life so she had no need of money from the insurance. The defence came back with the argument that he had never in fact honoured those payments. The jury convicted her of capital murder and asked the judge to be lenient with the sentencing. On September $2^{nd}$ 2014 after a sentence hearing lasting 5 hours the judge gave Tracey Grissom a 25 year prison sentence. She is liable for parole.

# LOUISE HARRIS

Born June 16<sup>th</sup>, 1953 - sentenced to death August 11<sup>th</sup>, 1989, this death sentence reversed on appeal October 2004. Awaiting re-sentencing.

Louise Harris is an African-American and was charged and convicted of arranging her husband's murder.

Harris had endured several years of a failed marriage to Isaiah Harris, a Deputy Sheriff in Montgomery County, Alabama. He had beat her regularly and she had sought solace and help in a relationship with Lorenzo McCarter with whom she confided about the physical and mental abuse and asked him to arrange a murder of her husband so they could be legally together. McCarter arranged with two friends, Michael Stockwell and Alex Hood to kill Harris on his way to work which they did using a 12 bore shotgun.

Stockwell was the one who fired the shots and being already on the police radar for armed assault was quickly picked up and told them McCarter was the instigator. McCarter was charged with capital murder and agreed to testify against Louise Harris to reduce his likely sentence to life in prison rather than the death penalty. Louise claimed she knew nothing about the plan to murder Isaiah.

Although Louise had a history of Post-Traumatic Stress Disorder, Battered Women's Syndrome and Dissociative Disorder they were never mentioned at her trial by her defence as mitigating circumstances. The jury at her trial recommended a life sentence which the

Alabama judge overrode and sentenced her to death. This was reversed on appeal and she awaits re-sentencing.

Hood and McCarter were both sentenced to life in prison without parole and Stockwell, the one who pulled the trigger was sentenced to death and sits on Death Row as his appeals roll on.

# AUDREY MARIE HILLEY

Born June 4th 1933 – sentenced to life in prison for the murder of her husband and attempted murder of her daughter in June 1983. Absconded from prison February 19th 1987 and died from hypothermia February 19th, 1987.

Audrey Hilley was born Audrey Frazier in the Blue Mountain neighbourhood of Anniston Alabama on June 4, 1933. Her parents were Huey Frazier and his wife, Lucille (née Meads). Audrey married Frank Hilley on May 8th, 1951; they had two children, Mike and Carol. Despite Frank's well-paying job and Marie's secretarial employment, the couple had little money set aside in savings due to Marie's excessive spending habits which led to tension in the marriage. Unbeknown to Frank, his wife frequently engaged in sex with her bosses in exchange for money or superior performance evaluations. He then began suffering from a mysterious illness, as did his son Mike, but Mike's symptoms, which his doctors attributed to stomach flu, abruptly stopped when he moved away from home to attend a seminary.

In 1975, after returning home early one day due to his illness, Frank found Marie in bed with her boss. He turned to son Mike, by then an ordained minister living in Atalanta for advice. In May 1975, shortly after a visit from Mike, Frank visited his doctor complaining of nausea and tenderness in his abdomen, and was diagnosed with a viral stomach ache. The condition persisted and he was admitted to a hospital where tests indicated a malfunction of his liver and doctors diagnosed infectious hepatitis. Frank Hilley died early in the morning of May 25, 1975.

Frank's autopsy, performed with his wife's permission, revealed a swelling of the kidneys and lungs, bilateral pneumonia, and inflammation of the stomach. Because the symptoms closely resembled those of hepatitis that was listed as his cause of death and no further tests were conducted. Frank had a moderate life insurance policy, secretly taken out by Marie at the time of his initial illness, that she redeemed for $31,140.

Three years later, Marie took out a $25,000 life insurance policy on her daughter Carol; a $25,000 accidental death rider took effect in August 1978. Within a few months, Carol began experiencing nausea and was admitted to the hospital emergency room several times. A year after filing the insurance policy on her daughter, Marie gave her an injection that she claimed would alleviate the nausea. However, the symptoms only worsened, with Carol enduring numbness in her extremities. After medical tests found no sign of a disease, Carol's doctor, fearing the symptoms were psychosomatic, had her undergo psychiatric testing at Carraway Methodist Hospital in Birmingham, Alabama. There, Carol secretly received two more injections from her mother, who warned her not to tell the doctors or nurses about the shots.

A month after Carol was admitted to the hospital, her doctor reported she was suffering from malnutrition and vitamin deficiencies, adding that he suspected heavy metal poison was to blame for the symptoms. Marie panicked incase tests were ordered and had Carol discharged from the hospital that afternoon. The following day, Carol was admitted to the University of Alabama Hospital. Coincidentally, Marie was arrested for bouncing worthless cheques which were written to the insurance company that insured Carol's life, causing that policy to lapse. At the hospital the doctors concentrated their investigation on the possibility of heavy metal poisoning, noting that Carol's hands and feet were numb, she had nerve palsy causing foot drop and she had lost most of her deep tendon reflexes.

The doctors also noticed Aldrich-Mees lines on Carol's nails. Forensic tests on samples of her hair were made by the Alabama Department of Forensic Sciences on October 3rd, 1979, revealing levels of arsenic ranging from over 100 times the normal level close to the scalp to zero times the normal level at the end of the hair shaft. This indicated that Carol had been given increasingly larger doses of arsenic over a period of four to eight months. That same day, Frank's body was exhumed, and upon examination, showed between ten and 100 times the normal level of arsenic. It was concluded that both Frank and Carol had suffered from chronic arsenic poisoning, with Frank's poisoning being fatal.

Marie was already in prison for her cheque bouncing charges when she was arrested on October 9th for the attempted murder of her daughter. Anniston police found a vial in her purse, in which tests revealed the presence of arsenic. Two weeks later, Frank's sister found a jar of rat poison which contained 1.4–1.5% arsenic. On November 9th she was released on bail, and registered at a local motel under an assumed name and then disappeared. While a note was left behind indicating that she "might have been kidnapped," Marie was listed as a fugitive.

On November 19th, a burglary occurred at the home of Marie's aunt. Her car was stolen as well as some clothes and an overnight bag. Investigators found a note in the house reading, *"Do not call police. We will burn you out if you do. We found what we wanted and will not bother you again."*

Two months later, on January 11th, 1980, Marie was indicted in absentia for Frank's murder. Subsequently, investigators found that both her mother and her mother-in-law, Carrie Hilley, also had significant, but not fatal, traces of arsenic in their systems when they died. The remains of Sonya Marcelle Gibson, an 11-year-old friend of Carol's who had died of indeterminate causes in 1974, were also exhumed and examined but were found to contain only a "normal" amount of arsenic. Gibson was one of the many neighbourhood children who had fallen ill after drinking beverages that they had been given during visits to the Hilley house. Two police officers who had been dispatched to a domestic disturbance at the Hilley house some time previously also reported coming down with nausea and stomach cramps after drinking coffee that Marie had offered them. Although police and the FBI launched a massive manhunt for her, Marie Hilley remained a fugitive for more than three years.

Using the alias "Robbi Hannon", Marie travelled to Florida and met a man named John Greenleaf Homan III. They lived together for more than a year before they married on May 29th, 1981, at which point she took his last name. The couple moved to New Hampshire. Late in the summer of 1982, she left New Hampshire, telling her husband that she needed to attend to some family business and to see some specialist doctors about an illness. During this time, she travelled to Florida and Texas using the alias "Teri Martin", an imaginary twin sister she had earlier told her husband existed.

During the trip, Marie called Homan pretending to be "Teri" and informed him tearfully that Robbi had died in Texas, saying there was no need for him to claim the body because it had been donated to medical science. After getting to know "Teri" over the phone, Homan expressed interest in meeting her. She agreed, saying they needed to put "Robbi's" death behind them. In November 1982, after changing her hair colour and losing weight, Marie returned to New Hampshire and reunited with Homan, posing as his "deceased" wife's twin sister Teri.

An obituary for Robbi Homan appeared in a New Hampshire newspaper, but aroused suspicion when police were unable to verify any of the information it contained. Homan's co-workers also had suspicions about his new "sister-in-law" Teri and were concerned fraud may have been at play. A detective with the New Hampshire State Police surmised that the woman living as Teri and Robbi were one and the same. Homan's concerned co-workers discovered that the Medical Research Institute of Texas, where "Robbi's" body was supposedly handed over for study, was non-existent, as was the church that eulogized her death.

While Homan's workplace was audited and no embezzlement found, authorities still believed that "Teri Martin" was possibly a fugitive bank robber named Carol Manning (later disproven) or wanted on other outstanding charges. In the meantime, "Teri" had taken a secretarial job in nearby Brattleboro, Vermont, and was arrested. While being interrogated by Vermont state troopers, she confessed that she was wanted in Alabama on the cheque fraud charges and divulged her true name. Contact with Alabama authorities confirmed this, while also disclosing the far more serious charges for murder and attempted murder. Marie was extradited to Alabama to stand trial. She was quickly convicted and sentenced to life in prison for her husband's murder and 20 years for attempting to kill her daughter.

Whilst serving her sentence in 1983 at the Julia Tutwiler Prison for Women in Wetumpka, Alabama, a maximum security prison, she was often assigned to perform paperwork, due to her clerical work background and was considered a quiet and model prisoner. This good behaviour earned her several one-day passes from prison, from which she always returned as scheduled.

In February 1987, Marie was given a three-day pass to visit Homan, who had moved to Anniston to be closer to her. They spent a day at an Anniston motel, and when Homan left for a few hours, she disappeared, leaving behind a note asking for his forgiveness. Homan promptly alerted police. Her escape prompted an inquiry into Alabama's parole policy.

Four days after she vanished from the motel, Marie was found delirious on the back porch of a house in Anniston. The woman who found her described her appearance as scary, stating she was dirty with mud on her face and long fingernails. Marie was conscious at the scene but lost consciousness while being transported to a nearby hospital for treatment. Upon arrival she suffered a heart attack. Doctors attempted to revive her but were unsuccessful, and she was pronounced dead $3\frac{1}{2}$ hours after being found. The coroner believed she had been crawling around in the woods, drenched by four days of frequent rain and exposed to temperatures that dropped to below freezing at night. Her final cause of death was attributed to hypothermia and exposure. She was buried by her children next to her husband Frank Hilley on February 28th, 1987. Why did Marie Hilley do the things she did? We will never know.

# RHONDA BELLE MARTIN

Born 1907 – executed by electrocution October 11th, 1957.

Because this case is fairly old the details available are pretty basic but it is here because of the rarity of a female serial killer murdering so many of her own family.

Rhonda Belle Martin was serial killer who was executed by the state of Alabama for the murder of Claude Carroll Martin, her fourth husband, in 1951. Martin's method of murder was rat poison. She was also accused of poisoning and murdering her own mother, as well as five of her seven children, all of whom were below the age of 12 at the time of their deaths. Only one of her victims, her former step-son and fifth husband Ronald Martin, is known to have survived. Although she initially confessed to all the murders she was accused of committing, she later recanted her confession in the murders of two of her children.

Martin's execution made her the third and final woman to be electrocuted in Alabama before the Furman v. Georgia ruling, as well as the last woman put to death in the state until 2002.

Rhonda Belle Martin née Thomley was born around 1907 in Alabama, to James Robert Thomley and Mary Frances. Prior to her arrest, she worked as a waitress. At the time of her arrest, she lived in Montgomery, Alabama.

She confessed in March 1956 to poisoning her mother, two husbands, and three of her children. She denied killing two other children. According to LIFE Magazine in an article published at the time, she loved getting the get-well cards, and matching them to the sympathy cards that came when the victims died.

Her fifth husband, Ronald Martin (formerly her step-son, as he was the son of Claude Carroll Martin), was poisoned like the others. However, he survived and was left a paraplegic. It was his illness that mystified the doctors and led law enforcement to take a long look into the strange deaths surrounding Rhonda Martin and her family.

Prosecutors said collecting insurance proceeds prompted her killing spree, although this is unlikely, since she collected only enough each time to cover burial costs.

Martin was convicted of murdering fifty-one-year-old Claude Carroll Martin in 1951 by slowly feeding him rat poison mixed into his meals. Although Martin was only convicted of one murder, she admitted to committing every murder she was suspected of, except for two of the children.

Because Martin had a heart condition, prison officials withheld information regarding her scheduled execution date until the day before her execution. Martin had a clemency hearing that lasted for two hours, during which her defence attorney unsuccessfully attempted to stop the execution on the grounds of Martin's sanity not having been adequately tested. She was housed in the Jefferson County jail until late May 1957 as her execution was set for May 31st, she was then transferred to Kilby Prison, where Alabama's electric chair was located at that time. When that execution date was postponed, she was sent to the Julia Tutwiler Prison for Women.

Eight days before her execution, Martin gave an interview in which she said, *'Well, you've never seen anybody who was happy to sit down in the electric chair. But if that's what it's got to be, that's what it will be.'* She was housed at the Julia Tutwiler Prison until approximately four hours before her execution time when she was then sent back to Kilby Prison.

On October 11th, 1957 Martin had a last meal consisting of a hamburger, mashed potatoes, cinnamon rolls, and coffee seven hours before going to the execution chamber. She was led to Alabama's electric chair while she held a Bible in her hand and was reported to be calm but quietly weeping as she recited the 23$^{rd}$ Psalm alongside the prison chaplain. She received the first shock at 12:10 am, and she was pronounced dead at 12:16 am and removed from the death chamber at 12:25 am. She had declined to make a final statement.

In 1956, Martin had expressed a desire for her body to be sent to an unspecified scientific institution for an autopsy report, so scientists could analyse her brain and find out why she committed her crimes. After her execution, prison officials found a note expressing a similar request. The note read that she wanted physicians *'to find out why I committed the crimes I committed. I can't understand it, for I had no reason whatsoever. There's definitely something wrong.'* After her execution, some family members received her body in a funeral home in Montgomery. No autopsy was performed.

Martin was the last woman executed in Alabama until 2002, when Lynda Block was executed for the murder of a policeman.

# JESSICA McCORD

Born 1971 – sentenced to life in prison without parole April 25$^{th}$, 2003.

Seven years after a bitter divorce that centred around the custody of their two daughters Jessica McCord and ex husband Alan Bates had both re-married. Jessica to a police officer in the Birmingham Alabama force and Alan to a co-worker in a Maryland theatre company.
In those seven years since the divorce Jessica had repeatedly tried to deny Alan access or visits to their two daughters now 12 and 10 years old. She had even gone as far as to move house several times, change telephone numbers and not responding to calls and letters.
On February 15$^{th}$ 2002 Alan and his wife flew to Birmingham from their Maryland home for Alan to have a meeting with Jessica at her lawyer's office to finalise any agreement about his visitation rights and sign a new custody agreement. It was agreed that Alan would take the girls back to Maryland for a few days. Later that afternoon he and his wife went to Jessica's house to pick the girls up relieved that all had been settled. Once there Jessica took them into the back room at the house where her police officer husband was waiting and shot them both several times killing both of them. The McCords then put into operation a plan they had devised to create an alibi for themselves. They visited a Home Depot store making sure they got timed receipts for goods bought and then bought cinema

tickets for that evening's performance of Lord of the Rings. They then put the Bates' bodies into the trunk of the Bates's rental car and drove several miles into Georgia before setting it on fire in rural Morgan County near Rutledge off the Interstate 20. The police were called to the scene by the landowner and at first thought it to be a car-jacking gone wrong. However once the child custody case was revealed suspicious police detectives decided to look more carefully into the case with the McCords attracting their attention.. They discovered that a partially burnt piece of cloth towel used to soak in petrol and light the gas drenched car had blown away from the vehicle and been collected by forensic scientists had a pattern that matched similar towels in the McCord's kitchen. A search of the McCord's home revealed that new floor tiles had been put down in part of the back room's floor and new wallpaper had been put on the walls so quickly that the pattern didn't align. Under the floor tiles were blood stains and behind the wall paper a hastily plastered over bullet hole in the wall contained a bullet and it matched those used to kill the Bates and all were fired from Officer McCord's police issue gun.

    The McCord's were arrested and charged on two counts of first degree murder. Jessica gave a tearful story to the jury about how Alan Bates had been a violent and awful husband and she was afraid of how he would treat the girls and might physically abuse them. It was all lies and the jury weren't fooled and on February 15th, 2003 gave a verdict of guilty of first degree murder times two. Her husband was also found guilty and both were given life in prison with parole after 25 years when sentenced on April 25$^{th}$, 2003.

# JUDITH ANN NEELLEY

Born 1964 – sentenced to death in Alabama on April 18$^{th}$, 1983. Commuted to life in prison on January 15$^{th}$, 1999. First became eligible for parole January 2014, denied. Denied again in 2018. Next hearing 2028.

Alvin Howard Neelley, Jr. (1953-2005) and Judith Ann Adams Neelley (1964-)were both convicted of the kidnappings and murders of Lisa Ann Millican and Janice Chatman. Judith Neelley was sentenced to death by the state of Alabama in 1983 with her sentence later commuted to life in prison in 1999. She is thought to be serving her sentence at the Julia Tutwiler Prison for Women in Wetumpka, Alabama. Alvin Neelley was serving a life sentence at the Bostick State Prison in Georgia where he died of natural causes in 2005.

Alvin Howard Neelley, Jr. was born in Georgia in 1953, where he was a known car thief from a young age. He met his second wife Judith Ann Adams when he was 26 years old and she was 15. Alvin divorced his first wife shortly before eloping with Judith in 1980.

Judith Ann Adams was born in Murfreesboro, Tennessee in 1964. Her father who was an alcoholic and died when she was nine. After meeting Alvin Neelley, she began her life of crime with him. Together they committed armed robbery across the country for which she was later caught. She gave birth to twins while incarcerated at Rome's Youth Development Centre.

On September 11, 1982, a Youth Development Centre worker, Ken Dooley's home was shot through four times. The following day, fellow employee Linda Adair's home was firebombed with a Molotov cocktail. Abusive phone calls were made to the victims following the attacks by a female who claimed to have been sexually abused at the Youth Development Centre, but neither victim could identify the caller's voice.

On September 25th, 1982, Lisa Ann Millican, a 13 year-old girl from Cedartown, Georgia was abducted by Alvin and Judith Neelley from the Riverbend Mall in Rome, Georgia. She was taken to a Murfreesboro, Tennessee motel where the Neelleys held her captive. Lisa was molested by both Neelleys, and Judith injected her with Drano drain cleaner. On the 28th, Lisa was shot in the head by Judith and her body was thrown into the Little River Canyon in Fort Payne, Alabama. Judith even called police three times to report where Lisa's body was to be found and boasted that more would follow.

Janice Chatman and John Hancock were a young engaged couple from Rome, Georgia. On October 4th, 1982, they were abducted by Judith Neelley. John Hancock was shot and left for dead while Janice Chatman was taken back to the Neelleys' motel room, where she was tortured and murdered. John Hancock, however, did not die, and was able to point out Alvin and Judith Neelley as his assailants when shown police mugshots.

Judith Neelley was arrested on October 9th, 1982, and Alvin a few days later. Judith was identified as being the perpetrator in the YDC employee attacks.

To avoid the death penalty, Alvin Neelley pleaded guilty to murder and aggravated assault in Georgia. He was not tried for the Lisa Millican murder.

Judith Neelley's trial began on March 7th, 1983. Before her trial she gave birth to a third child behind bars. After a six-week trial she was convicted of the murder of Lisa Ann Millican. The jury recommended a sentence of life in prison but judge Randall Cole thought that lenient and sentenced the 18 year-old mother of three to death in Alabama's electric chair.

Following her first conviction, Judith pleaded guilty to Janice Chatman's murder.

Alvin Neelley was kept at the Bostick State Prison from 1983 until his death in November 2005 from natural causes.

Judith Neelley became the youngest woman sentenced to death in the United States. She was on Alabama's Death Row at the Julia Tutwiler Prison for Women.

Judith appealed for a new trial, but it was denied in March 1987. In 1989, the United States Supreme Court affirmed her death sentence. On January 15th, 1999, Judith Neelley was days from her execution date when Alabama's then-governor Fob James granted her clemency and commuted her death sentence to life in prison. The decision was met with public outrage and legal controversy, but James cited how Judith's jury originally wanted to sentence her to life in prison, but the judge had sentenced her to death.

With the life sentence came the opportunity of parole as the Governor had not specified that the sentence be 'without parole'. At Neelley's 2018 parole hearing her lawyers argued that she had been coerced by her husband into committing the crimes. He was now dead and could not reject this claim but the parole board did and denied parole. The then current Governor sent in a request that parole be denied stating that he thought the previous Governor's reduction of the sentence from death to life was a mistake. In 2023 the parole board met again and denied parole. No legal representation was made on behalf of Neelley. Neelley's next parole board meeting is in 2028 when Neelley will be 64.

**END**

Thank you for buying/reading this book. I do hope you enjoyed it as much as I did doing the research. (although perhaps 'enjoy' isn't the right word!) To keep up with my new releases and other information on my talks, what book festivals I am attending and other useless information about me please become a friend on my Barry Faulkner Facebook page. I don't have a website, not enough time, but all my books are on my Barry Faulkner Amazon page together with the first pages of each as a taster. You can also order them at your local library or book shop if they don't have them already.

**DCS Palmer books (crime fiction)**
Future Riches
The Felt Tip Murders
Killer is Calling
Poetic Justice
Loot
I'm With The Band
Burning Ambition
Take Away Terror
Ministry of Death
The Bodybuilder
Succession
The Black Rose
Laptops Can Kill
Screen 4
Underneath The Arches

**Ben Nevis and the Gold Digger Series**
**(Private Eye thrillers)**

Turkish Delight
National Treasure
Chinese Takeaway
Double Trouble
The Pyramid

## True Crime Series
London Crime 1930s-2021
UK Serial Killers 1930-2021
UK Killers Vol 1. A to E.
UK Killers Vol 2. F to M.
UK Killers Vol 3. N to Z.
UK Female Killers
USA Killers Vol. 1. Alabama

## Others
Bidder Beware (Comedy crime)
Fred Karno (biography)

***************************